THE CONDUCTOR AS LEADER

*Principles of Leadership Applied
to Life on the Podium*

THE
CONDUCTOR
AS LEADER

*Principles of Leadership Applied to
Life on the Podium*

Ramona M. Wis

GIA Publications, Inc.
Chicago

To
my husband, one of the most respected "quiet leaders" I've known;
my daughter, that she may come to understand these principles
as she grows into her own leadership roles;
and
my parents, who showed me what serving was all about by
living it every day.

The Conductor as Leader
Principles of Leadership Applied to Life on the Podium

Ramona M. Wis

Copy editor: Gregg Sewell
Cover design and layout: Martha Chlipala

G-7071
ISBN - 978-1-57999-653-6

GIA Publications, Inc.
7404 South Mason Avenue, Chicago 60638
www.giamusic.com
Copyright 2007 GIA Publications, Inc.

Printed in the United States of America

TABLE OF CONTENTS ∼

ACKNOWLEDGMENTS ~~

I'm not sure if it takes a village or just a key group of influential people, but suffice it to say no accomplishment is the result of a single individual's efforts. Many people have played significant roles in my efforts to complete this project over the seven years that I have actively researched and written this book. My thanks go to:

North Central College for providing me fertile ground to grow my leadership skills and for the summer grants I received to study and write about leadership. A special thanks to my former colleague Roger Smitter, who introduced me to the ideas of Robert K. Greenleaf; and to my current colleagues Tom Cavenagh, for his guidance in the publishing process and Barbara Knuckles, a great people connector who helped me in seeking out publishers, as well as my colleagues in the arts who make going to work every day a real pleasure.

I am grateful to Larry Spears, Senior Fellow and President Emeritus of the Robert K. Greenleaf Center for Servant-Leadership for his input and guidance and my friends and supporters Mary Ann Kastner, Ariadne Moisiades, Cheryl Frazes Hill, Harris Fawell and Tim Lautzenheiser who were readers and encouragers of my work at various stages of this project. Your words and passion for this topic kept me plowing ahead in the tough times.

Thanks to my publisher, Alec Harris, my editor, Gregg Sewell and everyone at GIA for their excitement about this book and for all their help in the publishing process and to Sourcebooks, Inc. publisher Dominique Raccah for taking the time to steer me in the right direction and to acknowledge the credibility of this work.

I am indebted to the many influential writers and speakers from whom I have learned over the last several years, many of whom are included in this book and to my local Borders bookstore for providing a creative and relaxing environment for writers such as me (along with some darn good coffee).

Of course, I would not have had much to write about were it not for all the wonderful musicians I have had the pleasure to work with and lead over the past thirty years. The music we share, the challenges you present (and I mean that in a good way), and the laughter that ultimately results make life a very special adventure, indeed.

Finally, I thank my husband Brian, my daughter Alaina and all the members of my family for helping keep me sane, centered, and "real" and for helping me remember what's most important.

PROLOGUE
OPENING OUR EYES ~~

One of my favorite places to go when I have some free time is my local Borders bookstore. There's something about being in a relaxed environment, surrounded by thousands of books on every subject, that draws me to come back again and again and to keep picking up another new book.

It was on one of those harmless visits some twenty years ago that I picked up my first book on leadership. Truth be told, I'm not even sure which book it was. I just remember it was captivating, *not* written specifically for musicians and absolutely dead on when it came to laying out the challenges of leadership that, to my surprise, applied to my life as a conductor and teacher.

I have always been, as a good friend tells me, a student of process. Midway through my doctoral studies in music I seriously contemplated changing my major to educational psychology because I was fascinated (or frustrated) by observing how people function in learning environments, specifically the ensemble rehearsal. I had seen how musicians could achieve far beyond their innate talent level when the conductor set them up to succeed, but I had also seen how even the most gifted ensemble could suffer from low morale, lack of motivation and flat-lined expressiveness because the conductor seemed oblivious to or simply uninterested in the idea of designing a creative, engaging and edifying environment. I spent a lot of time studying, analyzing and experimenting with my own rehearsals to see how my teaching methods and ways of interacting with musicians affected the overall quality of the rehearsal and ultimately, the performance. As a supervisor and mentor for teachers I have had the opportunity to sit in on and analyze hundreds of instrumental and choral rehearsals and as a guest conductor I have worked with every size and ability level of ensemble under good and not-so-good conditions and always on a tight schedule. In short, I studied what made a conductor successful and taught what I learned to hundreds of students and teachers in undergraduate and graduate classes and conference workshops.

But it wasn't until I connected what I had read in that first serendipitous book to my own life as a conductor that I began to see what I really had been studying was *leadership*—specifically, *the way in which conductors use their skills, knowledge and character to create not only a fine musical product, but also a meaningful musical experience*. More than technique, more than knowledge, more than talent, more than personality—*leadership* is the key to great conductors and great ensembles.

THE CONDUCTOR AS AN ICON OF LEADERSHIP

For many, the words *conducting* and *leading* are synonymous, even outside of the music profession. Those interested in organizational leadership have historically cited the conductor/ensemble relationship as a model for the way successful organizations work: A strong, charismatic, autocratic leader with great skill and knowledge (the conductor) maps out a plan (rehearsal of repertoire to be performed) for the organization (the ensemble) and then sets about making it work. Along the way the leader uses inspiration (motivational talk and incentives) side by side with coercion (sarcasm, punitive extra rehearsals, threats to take away prized chairs) to make sure the job is complete. Almost any means justifies the end of an excellent product (a successful performance). This is a traditional, top-down approach to leadership and is an approach still followed by many organizations, musical and otherwise, today.

So what is there to talk about? This clearly defined model has been used for years and, while it's not perfect, it seems to work just fine. Why a book about leadership for the conductor?

Because more and more conductors are learning that organizational life—the way people work together to accomplish a collective goal—is changing and, as leaders of organizations, we need to respond to this change. In recent years, the move has been toward a flatter hierarchical structure, where followers (in our case, ensemble members) take on more responsibility and provide more input into many aspects of operations. The leader functions more as a coordinator of efforts, an expert guide who helps individuals achieve a mutually beneficial goal. There is greater involvement by all participants in the organization and theoretically, more accountability, leading to a deeper, more meaningful experience. Followers own the process more and therefore, feel more invested. Put simply, the focus is much less on ME versus THEM, much more on US.

You see, if I took everything I have learned about great leadership and boiled it down to one, overriding theme, it would be "It's not about me." It's not about what *I* can achieve or what kind of ensemble *I* can develop; it's about gaining an awareness of *what needs to be done to develop the people I am given to lead.* There has been a fundamental shift in thinking, a shift from ME to THEM; from a focus on position and power to one of leading by serving.

In our defense, conductors are seldom trained to make this psychological shift. After all, we spend most of our youth and educational training focused on ME: *my* feelings, *my* thoughts, *my* lessons, *my* grades, *my* study habits, *my* talent, *my* artistic development. It's all about ME. Then, almost overnight, we are conductors: trustees, really, of the musical lives of those who sing and play in our ensembles. All of a sudden, it's not about ME, it's about THEM. This requires a huge psychological jump. Few of us make the leap gracefully; some of us, never.

Whether or not we make this shift in our thinking determines the quality and direction of our entire careers. As we think, so shall we be, it has been said. If we are focused on ourselves, self-preservation kicks in and we make decisions based on our ego most of the time. How will it feel to *me*? What will work for *me*? How will *I* look to my various publics? How successful will *I* be? But if we shift our focus to those we lead, who are really those we *serve*, everything changes. We now ask, "What does the ensemble need to be successful? How can *we* work together to get there?"

Helping you understand how to make this shift is why I wrote this book.

WHAT WE LEARN FROM THE ORPHEUS PROCESS

Perhaps best known for its departure from a traditional, top-down organizational structure is the Orpheus Chamber Orchestra, known as the world's only "conductorless" orchestra. In *Leadership Ensemble*,[1] Orpheus executive director Harvey Seifter (with co-author Peter Economy) shows how the ensemble has functioned successfully for years precisely because it does *not* follow the traditional orchestral model of one dominant, autocratic conductor working with highly capable but largely silent musicians. Rather, Orpheus engages in a detailed organizational process that allows the members of the orchestra to participate in and take responsibility for everything from programming to marketing to score study and research to leading rehearsals and refereeing debates on artistic differences. The average tenure for Orpheus members is eighteen years and growing, presumably because they feel more empowered in Orpheus than in traditional orchestral settings.

---

1   Harvey Seifter and Peter Economy, *Leadership Ensemble: Lessons in Collaborative Management from the World's Only Conductorless Orchestra* (New York: Times Books, 2001).

For double-bass player Don Palma, a founding member, a brief foray into the world of conducted orchestras proved to be an experience that he didn't soon wish to repeat. Says Palma, "I took one year off from Orpheus at the very beginning and went to the Los Angeles Philharmonic. I just hated it. I didn't like to be told what to do all the time, being treated like my only value was just to sit there and be a good soldier. I felt powerless to affect things, particularly when they were not going well. I felt frustrated, and there was nothing I could seem to do to help make things better." As a member of Orpheus, however, life is quite different. In Palma's words, "Orpheus keeps me involved. I have some measure of participation in the direction the music is going to take. I think that's why a lot of us have stayed involved for so long."[2]

Few of us take the time to look at the traditional ensemble leadership model from the viewpoint of the individual musician, a model which can become more and more discouraging as one's knowledge and experience grows. Seifter and Economy describe it this way:

> A conductor communicates with the more than one hundred musicians "reporting" to him by standing on an elevated platform and waving a stick of wood at them. This communication is essentially one-way since individual musicians rarely—if ever—express an idea or opinion to the conductor. Orchestral musicians are constantly required to conform, and

---

2   Seifter and Economy, 26.

they are usually denied an individual sense of accomplishment. For example, in a traditional orchestra, an important element of the job of violinist number 26 is to make absolutely sure that his bow flies off the strings of his instrument at precisely the same nanosecond as violinists number 25 and number 27. If he does his job well, violinist 26's immediate feedback (and reward) is to be ignored by the conductor altogether. Creativity, engagement in the process, and employee satisfaction don't really enter into the equation.[3]

So compelling is their story that after examining the success and benefits of the Orpheus Process, the reader is left with the notion that the conductor is not only unnecessary, but in many ways a hindrance to artistic freedom and the achievement of musical goals.[4]

Are there but two choices: the dominant autocrat or the absence of a conductor altogether? I believe that neither extreme is necessary or even practical, at least for the great majority of musical ensembles that exist. However, from Orpheus we learn two critical points that will be built upon in this book: one, *that musicians feel a strong desire to be included in a more creative way than just following directions on cue.* They are capable of creative decision-making and want to be engaged in the process in order to feel fully invested in the music. There is a desire, even a need, to be involved when it comes to creating one's own musical destiny. As conductors we are typically not trained to think collaboratively when it comes to decision-making in the rehearsal and so for many of us this notion

---

3   Seifter and Economy, 20.
4   The authors of *Leadership Ensemble* were focused on the professional arena—professional ensembles and for-profit businesses. It is not clear whether they would advocate conductorless ensembles in every setting, such as public schools and churches.

seems foreign and perhaps threatening to our concept of what a conductor is and does.

At the core of this desire to be engaged more meaningfully in the creative process is the musicians' need to be seen and respected as a person rather than just the "third clarinet" or the "soprano section leader." Authentic relationships are fundamental to the musicians' sense of contribution and value and significantly impact their overall experience and creativity. Musicians also want to feel they are using their gifts in important rather than utilitarian ways and that they have opportunities to grow. In a cross-national study of symphony orchestras, Jutta Allmendinger, J. Richard Hackman, and Erin V. Lehman asked questions about job satisfaction, comparing responses with those of twelve other occupations, and found:

> For general satisfaction, orchestra players ranked seventh of the thirteen. And for satisfaction with growth opportunities, they ranked ninth—just below federal prison guards (although I hasten to add that we studied a very innovative prison) and just above operating room nurses and professional hockey players.[5]

A comment by a recently retired professional orchestral musician may be the most telling: "...this may look like a glamorous job, but it's not. It's a factory job with a little bit of art thrown in."[6] How ironic and unfortunate that those at the height of their creative abilities can feel so powerless to use their gifts in meaningful, satisfying ways.

---

5   J. Richard Hackman, from an address given at the University of Illinois School of Music Commencement Convocation, May 15, 2005. Published in *Sonorities*, a news magazine of the University of Illinois School of Music, Spring 2007.

6   J. Richard Hackman address, 2005.

The second but seemingly opposing point made clear as we look at the Orpheus Process is that *in any kind of musical ensemble, strong, visionary leadership is needed*. Whether the organizational structure of the ensemble is traditional or something very different, *someone* must make decisions about repertoire, study and present the music, lead the rehearsals, monitor the interpretive decisions and cue the ensemble at critical times during the performance of the piece, not to mention handle the many administrative tasks that are involved in performing organizations. There are also less tangible and equally important needs dealing with motivation, inspiration, conflict resolution and morale that have to be addressed. Whether these responsibilities are shared by several different people (as is the case with a "multi-conductored" ensemble, such as Orpheus—a truer description, I think) or handled by one primary conductor, someone must lead. And for the ensemble to reach its artistic potential and value the experience of making music the leadership must be informed and strong and have a clear, unified vision.

The Conductor as Leader

In writing *The Conductor as Leader* I had one main goal: to examine what we experience as conductors and teachers in light of what we can learn from some of the top authorities on leadership so we can determine foundational principles and apply them to our lives as leaders from the podium.

In researching this book I found that studying leadership apart from pedagogical or technical approaches to music can help illuminate universal principles and free us to reflect on how those principles can work for us as conductors. (It is like studying voice with a teacher of the opposite gender—you cannot directly copy your teacher's sound, so you are forced to focus on the underlying principles and apply those to your own technique.) Accordingly, the insights of Warren Bennis, Robert K. Greenleaf, Stephen Covey,

Jim Collins, John Maxwell, Ken Blanchard, Peter Drucker, James M. Kouzes, Barry Z. Posner and many other respected writers and researchers on leadership inform our exploration of leadership with meaningful insight also coming from conductors Daniel Barenboim and Benjamin Zander, as well as other musical sources.

The Conductor as Leader is a collection of reflection/action essays that urge you to do just that: *reflect* on your leadership and *take action* to improve it. Reflection and action must be paired and operate in balance: reflection pulls back; action plows ahead. Both are needed if change is going to happen.

We start our journey in Chapter I by looking at leadership: what it means, what misconceptions cloud our understanding, how we come to develop our leadership ability and how our leadership approach affects both the musical process and product.

In Chapters II through VI, we examine five spheres of leadership: Vision, Trust, Teaching, Persuasion and Character. In each chapter, we look at what constitutes that sphere, cover Keys or practical actions that you can take and end with reflections on the challenges unique to that area of leadership. In between chapters I have included Interludes, short conversations that help link together each topic by a commentary, an observation or an experience.

In Chapter VII, we consider what it means to lead for the long term—because learning about leadership and getting it right is a lifelong process. Finally, we close by challenging ourselves with a call to action as we move forward and look at a better, fuller, more musical way to lead from the podium.

WHO SHOULD READ THIS BOOK

The Conductor As Leader offers a comprehensive exploration of leadership and some practical ideas about how we can use our talents as conductors to be a significant part of a significant experience. This book is for any conductor who wants to better understand his role as a *leader* from the podium. It doesn't matter if you conduct university choirs or the community band or if you conduct by default because you are the general music teacher and beginning orchestra was part of the job (and you needed one). The principles in this book apply to all conductors and teachers who are willing to look hard at the way in which they live their professional lives. Regardless of your setting, these are fundamental principles that when applied can help you and the ensemble grow to the next level, to reach your goals and to accomplish this in a way that makes creating music in a community of musicians a rewarding experience—not just on good days but every day. If you want to grow as an artist who leads, if you want to understand how to make a significant difference in the lives of those you conduct and if you want to *enjoy* the process of developing excellent ensembles, then this book is for you.

And if you are not a conductor, you can also learn much about leadership through the principles explored here—principles that you can apply to your life, your work and your role as a leader. Whatever your motivation for reading *The Conductor as Leader*, my hope is that these essays will encourage you to reflect on your thinking and practice and help move you to the next stage in your development as a leader.

Warning: the life you change may be your own.

MAESTRO OR BOB?

I'll admit it: I love to watch reruns of classic sitcoms. One of my favorites is an episode of Seinfeld in which Elaine starts to date a new guy who seems to be a nice enough fellow except that he doesn't want to be called by his first name. He insists on being called Maestro. You see, he conducts a community band of sorts and as its conductor he expects to be regarded as one of the elite (like Maestro Bernstein, he points out). He takes every opportunity to remind those around him that he is in fact a Maestro: conducting passionately while he drives, singing Italian arias at the top of his lungs and funniest of all going completely stone-faced when someone, even girlfriend Elaine, innocently calls him ... *Bob*.

Maestro or Bob? An interesting question. To be a conductor is an awesome responsibility and a privileged job, one that often puts us in the public eye and one that demands professionalism, dedication and seriousness about our art.

But when it comes down to it, we are all Bob. We are people with strengths, weaknesses, passions, frailties, drives and fears. The Maestro in us puts up a marvelous front, but the Bob in us makes us vulnerable enough to look at ourselves authentically and realize that we have a way to go on the road to becoming better leaders.

If we put down the baton and allow ourselves to work on us instead of the next orchestral score, choral concert or marching competition we will find so much possibility that we haven't even begun to tap; possibility for us and for our ensembles, for exciting, creative, productive rehearsals and memorable performances.

So Maestro, enjoy these essays as I intended them: to be reflective, to call you to participate by applying the principles and practices to your life but also to be conversations between colleagues who have a shared history by virtue of the job we love. This is a book of encouragement, written as though we were sitting across the table from each other, exploring ideas and challenges about conducting, teaching, leading and working with people—over a good cup of coffee.

(Make mine decaf, Bob.)

CHAPTER ONE

THE JOURNEY BEGINS:

A LOOK AT LEADERSHIP ～

Fill in the blank: *The conductor's most important role is that of* _____. Timekeeper? Motivator? Musical pedagogue? Interpreter? Administrator? Teacher? Leader?

Ah, there it is. The "L" word. One of the most often used (and abused) terms there is. What does it mean to be a leader when it comes to the conductor?

At one level the answer is obvious—conductors lead by their technical ability, their musical knowledge and their personal charisma. They know how to get the job done, to get an ensemble prepared for a respectable performance. *How* they get to that performance varies from conductor to conductor, though the traditional model is one of an autocratic, sometimes dictatorial, presence that employs almost any means to ensure a good performance. A conductor with a domineering or temperamental personality is usually considered a strong leader just as a wall full of plaques from performance competitions or awards for professional recognition are regarded as evidence of a conductor's ability to lead.

But is this really what leadership is all about? Can a conductor's success as a leader be guaranteed by personality type or measured by hardware? Is the conductor's leadership ability evaluated solely by the end product: the performance? Or does the music-making experience have anything to say about the quality of the conductor's leadership?

This book is all about answering "Yes" to that question. Conductors are faced with fundamentally the same challenges as the CEO, pastor, parent or school principal. What distinguishes conductors is the kind of visibility we have, the way we express ourselves and share our talents and the way we use our leadership to create within a community of musicians.

As we begin an exploration into the leadership role of the conductor we need to look at the broader leadership picture. In this chapter we will explore common beliefs about leadership and ask you to reflect about the experiences you have had on both sides of the podium. We will clarify the difference between leading and managing and begin to examine the issue of power as we grow our understanding of what leadership really is. Finally, we will look at an approach to leadership that can help us as leaders from the podium create extraordinary experiences while creating extraordinary performances.

DEFINING LEADERSHIP—A STARTING POINT

While leadership is hard to describe in words, I believe John Maxwell's definition is a good place to start:

Leadership is influence—nothing more, nothing less.[7]

When we stand in front of an ensemble we exert our influence in multiple ways. The depth of the musicians' understanding and quality of their experience is a reflection of the way we lead rehearsals and performances. The value they place on music and music making is closely tied to how much they value us as the conductor of the

---

7   John C. Maxwell, *The 21 Irrefutable Laws of Leadership* (Nashville: Thomas Nelson Publishers, 1998), 17.

ensemble. The ensemble's openness to new ideas and new music is directly influenced by the way in which we model (or don't model) an attitude of openness. Their ability to be independent, thinking musicians capable of making creative decisions is shaped by the amount of responsibility we allow them to have. In short, our leadership as conductors is the sum total of our multi-faceted influence.

Curiously, many of us who conduct do not consider ourselves leaders. We assume leaders are those with titles, with positions of authority; that to be considered a leader, we have to have some degree of notoriety or the ensemble we conduct must be a professional or at least collegiate ensemble. Certainly a middle school music teacher with a lunchtime choir wouldn't be considered a *leader*, would he?

This all-too-pervasive mindset is the result of an incomplete or downright incorrect understanding of what leadership is. If leadership is influence, then we are all leaders because we all have influence. In fact, we have influence in multiple spheres—at school, at home, in the community, in our churches and with our musical ensembles. We all have known quiet leaders: people who by their very attitude and approach to life have taught us a great deal. They often were people without titles or big salaries but were powerful leaders and life-shapers nonetheless. Perhaps for you it was that middle school music teacher who influenced you so significantly that you chose music as your life's work. What greater evidence of influence—of leadership—is there?

> We have all met people in organizations with little or no positional power who daily influence others to be more enthusiastic, more committed, and more willing to be the best they can be. Again, one of the operative words in our leadership definition is the ability to *influence* others for good.[8]

---

8   James C. Hunter, *The World's Most Powerful Leadership Principle: How to Become a Servant Leader* (Colorado Springs, CO: WaterBrook Press, 2004), 34–5.

If leadership is influence, then each of us has the ability to lead every day by who we are, what we do and what we say. Whenever we interact with people we have the opportunity to influence them—lead them—in some way. The question is: how do we use that influence?

THE DIFFERENCE BETWEEN LEADING AND MANAGING

In order to use our influence in the fullest way we need to understand the difference between leading and managing. Put simply, *managing is about tasks, things and efficiency, while leading is about people, effectiveness and growth.*

Robert P. Neuschel describes the difference between a leader and manager, first quoting Webster's Unabridged Ditionary and then using James MacGregor Burns' distinctions *transactional* and *transformational* leader:

> Manager: "One who conducts business affairs with economy—with efficiency." (James MacGregor Burns would describe this role as transactional, that is, carrying out the business at hand under the existing general framework.) Leader: "One who goes before to guide or show the way…"(Burns refers to this role as transforming because it may involve moving in a different direction or changing cultures or method of operation.[9]

Recognized authority on leadership Warren Bennis provides a side-by-side comparison of the attributes of the manager vs. those of the leader:

9   Robert P. Neuschel, *The Servant Leader: Unleashing the Power of Your People* (East Lansing, MI: Vision Sports Management Group, Inc., 1998), 41–42.

4

- The manager administers; the leader innovates.
- The manager is a copy; the leader is an original.
- The manager maintains; the leader develops.
- The manager focuses on systems and structure; the leader focuses on people.
- The manager relies on control; the leader inspires trust.
- The manager has a short-range view; the leader has a long-range perspective.
- The manager asks how and when; the leader asks what and why.
- The manager has his eye always on the bottom line; the leader has his eye on the horizon.
- The manager imitates; the leader originates.
- The manager accepts the status quo; the leader challenges it.
- The manager is the classic good soldier; the leader is his own person.
- The manager does things right; the leader does the right thing.[10]

The main distinction between leading and managing is the amount of growth or change that occurs in the people and organizations we lead. Managers keep current operations running smoothly; leaders are always looking for ways to provide growth and development. The conductor who manages the ensemble is focused on getting a respectable concert program ready in the most efficient and orderly way possible; the conductor who leads the ensemble goes further and is focused on the process of making music and the musical experience, the technical and expressive growth of the individuals as well as the ensemble as a whole and the

---

10   Warren Bennis, *On Becoming a Leader* (Cambridge, MA: Perseus Books, 1989), 45.

development of the entire musical organization. The difference is enormous though not always evident at first. Good managers are often viewed as good leaders because they consistently get things done well and on time. This ability is valuable and often rewarded by retention, tenure, promotions, recognition or offers for more prestigious conducting posts. *But by itself effective management does not constitute great leadership.*

As conductors our inability to distinguish management from leadership has much to do with our professional training. Undergraduate and graduate music degree programs almost exclusively focus on developing one's ability to manage the musical ensemble. Courses in methods, conducting, pedagogy and even classroom management help future conductors find appropriate ways to organize the musical experience in an efficient manner. Clinical experiences, internships, student teaching, and seminars all focus on honing necessary managerial skills until finally we are released into the world to begin a career. But while being a good manager is a necessary skill for the conductor, it is not sufficient if the conductor is truly going to lead the ensemble.

For most people managing is easier than leading, especially if they are task oriented persons. (No names, please.) Tasks don't have opinions; things don't have feelings; your to-do list doesn't have emotional crises or personality conflicts. While managing includes the human factor, leading is *all about* the human factor. This is not to diminish the importance of being a good manager or administrator; it is simply to underscore how easy it is to fall into the trap of thinking that organizing events, tasks and even people into efficient modes of operation constitutes leadership. Remember, when we deal with tasks, we are managing; when we move to the realm of influencing people, we begin to talk about leadership.

Understanding the difference between managing and leading is crucial if we are to get better at both and incorporate the strengths of each into our conducting lives. Many of the ideas in this book will help you blend managing with leading, to make administrative decisions based not only on what works efficiently but on what will improve the relationships and experiences you and your ensemble enjoy.

AUTHORITY DOES NOT EQUAL LEADERSHIP

In the same way that managing can be mistaken for leading, authority and the power that comes with it can be mistaken for leadership.

Having a position or title along with the right to make decisions that others must abide by seems to be the primary office of the leader. But just as managerial ability is necessary but not sufficient for great leadership, having authority is but one component of a much broader spectrum of leadership responsibilities.

There are many people in positions of authority who are not good leaders. (Admittedly not a news flash, but it is worth pausing here to ponder the obvious.) Take a moment to think about a person you have known that had authority over you (a conductor, teacher, parent, boss) but who handled this responsibility poorly. Perhaps they made random, careless or inconsistent decisions, creating an inequitable and hence bitter work environment. Maybe they used their position of authority to pressure or coerce you in a selfish way or to make you feel guilty for their own inadequacies. Whatever the case, these authorities never realized their optimum leadership role or ability but rather focused on power itself. It doesn't matter what title they may have had; they were not leaders in the truest sense of the word.

Now think of a leader who used his leadership role and the authority that went along with it to improve the lives of those he led. Instead of "throwing his weight around" he pitched in alongside his followers to get the job done. He may have sacrificed personal comfort or notoriety so that the group could reach its potential. And when the applause came (if it came), he was the first one to give it away.

Authority and leadership are not synonymous. Though leaders often have titles and the authority to make decisions, those in authority can be lousy leaders. Being hired as Chair of Orchestral Studies doesn't guarantee your excellence as a leader, just the authority to influence. *How* you use that influence will ultimately define your effectiveness as a leader.

What we are really talking about is the distinction between formal (or positional) and informal authority. In his book *Social Intelligence: The New Science of Success*, Karl Albrecht defines the difference:

> Formal authority, obviously, comes with position power—someone or some entity, such as a president or prime minister, a governor, a mayor, a board of directors, or an electorate—has anointed you formally and has granted you a certain range of authority. Earned authority, on the other hand, does not come from others in power positions; you get it from other people, one at a time. You can earn authority by behaving in ways that cause others to consider you worthy of the right to influence them.[11]

We want to develop the ability to earn authority with people rather than focus on acquiring positional authority for the sake of the title or power that comes with it. Unless we understand the distinction and the need to center our energies on earned authority, our leadership ability will be compromised.

The challenges conductors face in this area are so important that I have devoted an entire chapter to their discussion. Authority,

---

11   Karl Albrecht, *Social Intelligence: The New Science of Success* (San Francisco, CA: Jossey-Bass, 2006), 226.

8

power, control and coercion are serious matters because they can so easily blind us to our ability to lead well. I remember reading somewhere that the real strength of our character is tested not by adversity but by how well we handle power. As conductors we take this test every day.

True leadership goes beyond managing people to growing them; true leadership recognizes authority as an opportunity to lead, not as a license to rule others. The conductor who wants to lead well recognizes these distinctions and as we will see, understands the importance of relationships: with the ensemble, the public and with the music. In short, conductor-*leaders* are keenly aware of their multi-faceted influence and strive to use this influence to improve the lives of all they encounter.

CHOOSING OUR APPROACH TO LEADERSHIP

If we use our influence in the most positive way—focusing on the needs of the individual musicians as well as the ensemble, and on the integrity of our art—we are leading by serving. This approach to leadership, known as servant leadership, has at its core the fundamental question "How can I help?" *How can I help the individual musicians grow as technicians and expressive artists? How can I help them be independent musical decision-makers? How can I help the ensemble understand this music and develop a beautiful sound? How can I help develop this organization to the next step and help audiences enjoy the music we perform? How can I help parents, administrators and everyone in my sphere of influence understand the importance of music in our lives?*

The term servant leadership seems like a paradox. For many the word servant automatically conjures up negative images because it is often associated with lack of ability or initiative, a weak personality, lower intelligence or skill and a lower position. Service occupations such as nursing or police work are appreciated but not always highly regarded or compensated. Serving (as in the military or in volunteer

9

positions) is admirable but not particularly enjoyable or financially profitable. All in all, the notion of serving is rarely enthusiastically embraced when understood only in these contexts.

It is unfortunate that in our collective psyche serving has gotten such a bad reputation. If leaders influence others, they do so by their actions. Their actions, when well intentioned, crafted and delivered, help make any situation better. Helping our musicians understand or perform music at a higher level is a form of serving and, I believe, a significant form of serving.

Servant leadership is about using your unique skills, talents, passion and knowledge in a way that improves the lives of those around you and in so doing improves and enriches your own life as well. Serving means being a conduit between two entities whose potential can only be fully realized when they are linked by what you can provide. The music on the page has enormous potential; so do the musicians in front of you. When conductors act as conduits to help or serve both the music and the musicians everyone moves closer to realizing their potential and the music comes alive.

Serving the musicians who are entrusted to you does not necessarily mean giving them what they want. Rather, you strive to give them what they *need*. The musicians may want the day off because they are struggling with a challenging piece; you realize that what they need is a fresh, new approach to understanding and rehearsing it. They may want to converse excessively during rehearsal; you know they need a faster pace and higher quality literature to stimulate them and keep them focused. They may want to program music they know; you believe they need to explore new territory. Servant leaders don't abdicate their responsibility by pandering to everyone else's whims; they assess the situation by listening, reflecting and using their skills and knowledge, then make a decision that supports the overall vision of the organization. When servant leaders ask "How can I help?" they are really asking "How can I help *meet their needs?*"

Servant leadership is a way of thinking about leading. It is not a checklist of tasks or methods that once accomplished qualifies you as a "member of the club." Servant leadership is reflective and engaging; strong leadership that has at its core the desire to help others meet perhaps their most significant need: their need to grow and contribute meaningfully to an organization and an ideal.

> In the end, being a servant-leader is not something you *do* but rather something you *are*. It is about creating the right environment to get the best out of people and unleash their true potential. Servant-leadership should not be misinterpreted as soft management—some of the most tough-minded leaders today are firm believers in and exponents of servant-leadership. Far from it, it is about effectiveness and there is clearly a need![12]

REFLECTING ON SERVANT LEADERSHIP

Servant Leadership, while not a new concept, has in the last few decades been studied and promoted by many as a leadership philosophy or approach. Most often credited with bringing servant leadership to the forefront in recent years is the late Robert K. Greenleaf. Following a successful career in business, Greenleaf launched a new career upon retirement when he actively researched, wrote about and taught servant leadership. In his seminal essay entitled *The Servant as Leader*, Greenleaf describes the essence of the servant leader:

> The servant-leader *is* servant first.... It begins with the natural feeling that one wants to serve, to serve

---

12 Don DeGraaf, Colin Tilley, and Larry Neal, *Servant-Leadership Characteristics in Organizational Life* (Indianapolis, IN: The Greenleaf Center for Servant-Leadership, 2001), 27–28.

first. Then conscious choice brings one to aspire to lead. That person is sharply different from one who is *leader* first, perhaps because of the need to assuage an unusual power drive or to acquire material possessions. For such it will be a later choice to serve—after leadership is established...

The best test, and difficult to administer, is: Do those served grow as persons? Do they, *while being served*, become healthier, wiser, freer, more autonomous, more likely themselves to become servants? *And*, what is the effect on the least privileged in society; will they benefit, or, at least, not be further deprived?[13]

"The servant leader is servant first." Think back to your early musical experiences. What motivated you in those early years? Competition? Love for music? Duty (your parents forced you into lessons)? Desire to be involved in something your friends were involved in? Perhaps a combination of these?

Now think of your first leadership position in music. It may have been as a section leader or as a student officer of an ensemble. Maybe you were the drum major of your marching band. What led you into that position? How did you view your role in those early years as you stood in front of the ensemble and performed as a leader?

For some of us there was a definite desire to serve. I remember serving as choir librarian during my high school years. This was a job I took very seriously, going so far as to spend the better part of one summer reorganizing and cataloging the entire choral library and then writing a manual for future librarians so they could perform the job with as much ease and clarity as possible. I did this because I wanted to help and because I knew I had organizational abilities

---

13   Robert K. Greenleaf, *Servant Leadership: A Journey into the Nature of Legitimate Power and Greatness* (New York: Paulist Press, 1977), 13–14.

that could make a difference. A shy vocalist at that time, I felt that sharing my administrative skills was my unique way of making a difference in the choral program. It was leading by serving.

Maybe you recall similar situations, times where you really wanted to be involved in something you cared passionately about and therefore were eager to share whatever talents you had. As adults many of us find ourselves in leadership positions in professional organizations and looking back, realize it started the very same way. We had a concern or saw a need so we volunteered, believing we could make a positive difference. Our efforts and success were recognized and before we knew it, we were elected or appointed to a higher, more prestigious position. Because of our initial service we found ourselves not only in a position of leadership but perhaps also in a position with a prestigious title and a high degree of authority.

But something happens along the way. Somewhere amid the busy, complicated and mysterious interweaving of life events we can begin to find ourselves seeking out positions with titles and authority not because we want to help or to serve but because *we are intrigued by the title or the authority itself*. We imagine ourselves holding a conducting post, a teaching job or a board position in an organization and contemplate how important it will make us. We begin to "believe our own press" and become drawn to the power and prestige that may accompany the position while forgetting our real purpose for being there. Because we overestimate our abilities and underestimate the time it takes to accomplish things well we take on too many jobs, ultimately leaving a mess in our wake. We find ourselves devoting the majority of our time to auxiliary positions that bring us prestige (at least in our own mind) while right under our noses our primary responsibilities are suffering. We can, unfortunately, begin to forsake our leadership because we simply stop serving.

This book will challenge us to examine our leadership lives, to stop long enough to recapture that first desire to make a difference and serve though our art. To remember those first profound moments with music; to understand how we as conductors can choose to be an open, inviting doorway between the music and the musicians instead of a wall too intimidating to scale. To remember or to learn for the first time what it means to be a conductor who is a servant leader.[14]

APPLYING SERVANT LEADERSHIP AS CONDUCTORS

"The best test, and difficult to administer, is: Do those served grow as persons? Do they, while being served, become healthier, wiser, freer, more autonomous, more likely themselves to become servants?" As conductors, we are entrusted with the growth of those who sing or play in our ensembles. Their skills, knowledge and experience are equally important considerations. We can not simply focus on developing their abilities as singers or players; we must also help them understand the creative process from the inside out so that they can move from being musical *for* us, to being musical *with* us, to ultimately, being musical *without us*. Even if they spend the rest of their lives as members of ensembles under someone's direction, what we should want for the musicians we lead is their ultimate independence: their ability to think and perform musically, to know what musical decisions need to be made when faced with a score and to have the ability to make them. Their growth as autonomous musicians is what we should strive for.

Conductors who choose to use their position of influence to serve surrender to a higher calling. As servant leaders this calling means serving our musicians and our organizations but it also refers to serving our art: music. What we do in our rehearsals eventually

---

14   If the concept of servant leadership is new to you, I recommend a simple, but powerful book called *The Servant* by James C. Hunter. This is a story that illustrates in real-world ways what servant leadership is all about. I also recommend reading Larry Spears essay on "The Ten Characteristics of Servant-Leadership" which can be found on the Greenleaf Center website *www.greenleaf.org*. There is no manual for servant leadership, but these can help you begin to understand the thinking behind the perspective on life and leading that servant leadership embodies.

leads to a performance, one that we hope will be glorious quite simply because the music deserves no less. My experience in talking to conductors is that all of them started on this career path because of their deep connection to and love of music. At some point in our lives we had an almost spiritual experience with music. It may have been as a performer or a listener, young or not so young, but whatever it was it was powerful. Music became at that moment other-worldly, taking us to a higher place. Now, as conductors, we aspire to bring others with us to that higher place, but to do so means we must think outward, away from our egos and toward something greater than any one individual. When we commit to this kind of leadership, everyone—conductor, ensemble and audience—reaps the benefits.

BECOMING A BETTER CONDUCTOR-LEADER

At this point you may be thinking "Who knew leadership was so complicated? Is all this really necessary? After all these years how can I change my thinking, my methods and my approach? Is it even possible to change?"

The bad news: becoming a great leader is a choice few will make. The good news: leadership can be learned. While leadership can't be reduced to a set of tasks that are mechanically completed, it does involve skills that can be developed if we have the will and desire to grow.

> Leadership is not a place, it's not a gene, and it's not a secret code that can't be deciphered by ordinary people. The truth is that leadership is an observable set of skills and abilities that are useful whether one is in the executive suite or on the front line, on Wall Street or Main Street, in any campus, community, or corporation. And any skill can be strengthened, honed, and enhanced, given

the motivation and desire, the practice and feedback, and the role models and coaching.[15]

You may believe as I did that "there are leaders and there are followers." Let's face it: some people just seem to have a knack for leading; they are successful, well liked, effective—it all just seems to work for them. Others struggle. They not only get little done for the organization, but they seem to have more personality conflicts and are not well thought of by their peers or the people who work under them. They lack charisma (even personality) and direction. Still others are verbally caustic and sarcastic in their roles, abusing their position at the expense of others. Why then is there such a disparity if everyone can learn to lead?

While answering that question could fill a book of its own, I believe that fundamentally there are requisites for leadership that must be in place if we are to become true leaders. Without these we may appear professionally successful on the surface but may never realize the full impact we could have made on the lives of those around us. Our titles, academic degrees and even bankbooks may be impressive but our souls will be lacking.

The first requisite for leadership is a passion for one's work and the professional skills to match. We must have passion or a deep love for music if we are to even hope to be great leaders of music. Passion fuels our vision and provides the energy we need to keep moving forward. Passion inspires our artistry and our teaching; passion makes the difference between a technically accurate performance and a musically alive experience.

Unfortunately, the demands of the job, our hectic schedules and the lack of variety we often inflict upon ourselves can dampen the joy we knew in our earlier years. But that joy can return if we remember what drew us to music in the first place and if we commit to re-engaging with music in meaningful ways.

---

15   James M. Kouzes and Barry Z. Posner, *Leadership Challenge*, 3rd ed. (San Francisco, CA: Jossey-Bass, 2002), 386.

Passion, to really make a difference, must be coupled with musical skill. All the fervor in the world will not help if our basic musical skill and knowledge are lacking. While each of us has strengths and weaknesses, we should not use our charisma to hide fundamental inabilities. Leaders are role models in every way, not the least of which is their demonstrated scholarship through artistry.

The second fundamental requisite for leadership is a genuine concern for people. Unless we really care about the individuals who sit in front of us we will never be true leaders because our focus will be on product at the expense of process. As conductors we are constantly faced with time constraints, demanding schedules and music that just refuses to come together. How do we respond to those pressures? If our main concern is the people we lead, we will make decisions that will preserve their integrity and experience while moving us closer to a fine musical performance. If our main concern is the musical product, we can unthinkingly say and do things that endanger morale, respect and ultimately, expressive music making. This is not to say that life will be free of conflict or that we will never make mistakes; nor does it mean that we must resist lighting a fire under the ensemble at those crucial times. It means laying a foundation—from the earliest decisions about organizational structure and repertoire, to the scheduling of rehearsals and concerts, right through to the rehearsals themselves—that limits the pressures in the first place and allows for adaptability when life dictates.

The third fundamental requisite is a desire to become a leader. As with anything in life, we must study leadership if we are truly to begin to understand it. Because so many of our ideas about leadership have been unconsciously absorbed from our own experiences—from our teachers, conductors and mentors—we are often unaware of the source of our own actions. We rarely examine our leadership approach to see if it fits our personality and core beliefs. We must first take the time to discover our professional philosophy as it relates to our lives as conductors, and then seek out ways to learn more about the fundamental principles and challenges of leadership.

Finally, if we are to become a leader in the fullest sense of the word *we must be willing to look inward at our character—our beliefs, attitudes, motivations, fears and personality—and how it fuels our actions.* Whether we realize it or not, *who* we are always comes out in *what* we do. We may be able to function smoothly when life is good but as soon as the pressure is on (and it will be) our true selves emerge. It is precisely at these moments that our ensembles look to us for leadership; whether we can provide it is a matter of character and integrity.

The bad news: leadership can't be learned in a day, in a weekend or through a seminar or a book. The good news: we *can* become better leaders starting today. And though becoming a leader is a lifelong journey, not a destination, there are real markers—turning points—where we become aware that we are on the right track; that we are making a difference, focusing our efforts in the right direction, paying more attention to what really matters and living life with real purpose. How do we begin to make this change? How do we grow from conductor as manager to conductor as leader?

> Once [managers] discover their purposeful potential, they are transformed from managers to leaders. It's important to note that no personality change is necessary. What is required is a commitment to discover purpose and to grow to a new level of personal potential and expression.... [I]t's all about living our life congruent with our principles, beliefs, and character.... [I]t's about living "on-purpose."[16]

Living "on purpose" means making the decision to be who you are; to have the courage to follow your own instincts and use your gifts. It's about knowing yourself.

---

16 Kevin Cashman, *Leadership from the Inside Out* (Provo, UT: Executive Excellence Publishing, 1999), 68.

By the time we reach puberty, the world has reached us and shaped us to a greater extent than we realize. Our family, friends, school, and society in general have told us—by word and example—how to be. But people begin to become leaders at that moment when they decide for themselves how to be.[17]

Our music and our ensembles deserve conductors who are "on purpose" in their leadership. Decide today to find and develop the leader in you.

---

17   Bennis, 1989, 53.

To the Skeptics,

the Cynics

and the Realists ~~

(You Know Who You Are)

Much of what is written in this book will challenge you, even to just keep reading as you come across ideas that seem counterintuitive to everything you believe about being a conductor. Your knee-jerk reaction may be "Well, maybe with college students who *want* to be there," "Sure, if everyone is nice, talented, and motivated, but in the *real world...*" or "Well, it's not like that when you work with *professionals*."

These and other thoughts will creep into your thinking. I know, because they have crept into mine as I have read the words of others and tested their ideas, especially when I have been in a particularly challenging time with my own ensemble or in my own conducting life. Conflicts, setbacks and a career sprinkled with less-than-perfect conducting environments can be heavy influences, coloring our thinking without our even realizing it.

It is easy to dismiss possibility by shutting our eyes to it, by criticizing another's viewpoint as unrealistic and naïve or at least impractical in most settings. But ask yourself: *Is everything in your organization ideal?*

Unfortunately, human nature (or maybe, the process of living life) causes us to see things in absolute dichotomies. We can only envision two options: either the completely autocratic, strong-willed conductor who would never think of asking musicians for input lest she appear weak, incapable or too docile for the job or the good-natured, grandmother/grandfather type who never wants to ruffle feathers and always wants to make people happy.

Why can't we see that much of life's possibilities lie in a third option: a large ocean of blended abilities and sensitivities, intuitions and sharpened skills, flexible and malleable working scenarios, entrepreneurial spirit and people-savvy leaders? Why don't we understand that real change, growth or influence only exists in this region of awareness and choice?

If we were to imagine the ideal conductor we would certainly start with a skilled, knowledgeable musician. But beyond that, wouldn't we also envision a conductor who has the ability to make rehearsals interesting relative to the age and ability level of the ensemble? Who has a sense of humor to lighten the tension of difficult repertoire and a demanding workload? Wouldn't we want a conductor who respects himself and others and is open to multiple ideas and perspectives while still being able to make excellent and timely decisions? Don't we want to know that a conductor has integrity on and off the podium? And wouldn't we want to be inspired by an authentic passion for music and the musical life, a passion that carries us along like a swift current in very pleasant waters?

If this is what we can envision—whether or not we are that conductor (yet) or know a conductor who fits this bill—then that vision can and should be our driving force in making it a reality. Our own history does not have to dictate the future, though it can be a reference for us as we *build* the future.

It's okay to be a skeptic. I have kept us very much on the page as I have written every word, challenging myself to think of life in practical terms as I share these principles and ideas. Just don't let your skepticism block you from becoming the conductor you can be.

CHAPTER TWO

LEAD WITH VISION ~⌒

Does anybody see what I see?

—John Adams,
in the musical *1776*

Vision. What an overused word these days. We talk of casting vision for our organizations, writing vision statements. We describe someone as having vision or being a visionary and criticize people for having tunnel vision. Why all this talk about *vision?*

Vision refers to the ability to see, in this case, figuratively. "To form a mental picture of; to understand; to imagine as having the character or capacities necessary for some specified activity."[18] Someone who has vision has the ability to see potential, to imagine possibility, often in contrast with those around her who are "blind": unable to see potential or who refuse to look for these same things.

Vision means setting goals, targets to shoot for. Leaders are able to set goals for themselves and for those they lead and they have the ability to help others see and move toward those goals. Leaders provide direction and purpose.

---

18   *The New Lexicon Webster's Dictionary of the English Language* (New York: Lexicon Publications, Inc., 1989).

> A mark of leaders…is that they are better than
> most at pointing the direction. As long as one is lead-
> ing, one always has a goal…. [T]he leader always knows
> what it is and can articulate it for any who are unsure.
> By clearly stating and restating the goal the leader
> gives certainty and purpose to others who may have
> difficulty in achieving it for themselves.[19]

Vision is a critical topic in books on corporate leadership and management because with all the tasks and pressures it is easy for leaders to get caught up in the everyday, shortsighted, right-in-front-of-your-nose details that they can't see the bigger picture. We become focused on what Stephen Covey calls the "urgent but not important" and seldom get around to the really significant things in life. Or, because we fail to take the time to plan and think long-term, we find ourselves regularly operating in a state of crisis, adding to our stress levels and creating anxiety for everyone around us.[20]

For the conductor vision means many things. As leaders we are charged with the long-term welfare of our organizations: what they accomplish throughout the season and from year to year. More than just preparing for the next concert, we need to have a long-term sense of where we are going as a musical ensemble and as an

---

19 Greenleaf, 1977, 15.
20 Stephen R. Covey, *First Things First* (New York: Simon & Schuster, 1995). In chapter two, "The Urgency Addiction," Covey includes a Time Management Matrix consisting of four quadrants: I (Urgent and Important), II (Important but Not Urgent), III (Urgent, but Not Important), and IV (Not Urgent and Not Important). Of Quadrant I, Covey says "…many important activities become urgent through procrastination, or because we don't do enough prevention and planning." Quadrant II is where we do our long-range planning, anticipate and prevent problems, empower others, broaden our minds and increase our skills through reading and continuous professional development, envision how we're going to help a struggling son or daughter, prepare for important meetings and presentations, or invest in relationships through deep, honest listening. Increasing time spent in this quadrant *increases our ability to do.*" Quadrant III is the "Quadrant of Deception. The noise of urgency creates the illusion of importance. But the actual activities, if they're important at all, are only important to someone else." Quadrant IV is the "Quadrant of Waste," time-wasting activities that have no restorative value (p. 37).

organization: we need a sense of purpose, a set of goals and a long-term plan for achieving them.

Conductors also utilize visionary ability in the short term, as in the next few weeks leading to a concert or for the rehearsal this afternoon. Though more commonly thought of as planning or preparing, this kind of vision is just as critical to the success of the ensemble because it is immediately realized. The well-led rehearsal today creates a sense of momentum and builds relationships that can be the building blocks toward achieving more long-term goals. (We'll discuss this kind of planning vision in Chapter V.)

Vision allows us to meld our artistic imagination with our strategizing ability to develop a kind of road map to success. Without vision we are in danger of leading fragmented lives, full of busyness without fulfillment. We can become locked in a kind of perennial state of *déjà-vu*, eventually exhausted by the feeling that we have been here before, so what's the point? Vision ensures that we are leading and not just existing in our role as conductors.

> Leadership is an influence process in which you try to help people accomplish goals. All good leadership starts with a visionary role. This involves not only goal setting but also establishing a clear picture of perfection—what the operation would look like when it was running effectively. In other words, leadership starts with a sense of direction.[21]

EVERYTHING STARTS WITH A DREAM

For us to have that sense of direction Blanchard talks about we need to allow ourselves to dream. Vision is built on a dream, on

---

21   Ken Blanchard, "Servant-Leadership Revisited" in *Insights on Leadership: Service, Stewardship, Spirit, and Servant-Leadership*, ed. by Larry C. Spears (New York: John Wiley & Sons, Inc.), 1998, 22.

asking ourselves questions such as "What is our artistic potential?" "Who will we be?" "What musical niche will we fill?" "How can we fulfill our responsibilities (to students, administrators, boards, audiences) in the most creative and fulfilling way?" "What is my unique place in the life of this organization?"

Dreaming is the seed of vision. Far from being soft stuff, dreaming is the act of unleashing possibility in our minds, the place where all great things start. Nothing great was ever accomplished without a great dream. We sometimes cut ourselves off from dreaming, telling ourselves to get real. But what does getting real get us? Stunted growth, self-imposed limits, mediocrity and routine, shortsightedness and closed hearts. These may be real, but only because so many people have stopped dreaming, *not* because they are inevitable. We need to give ourselves permission to dream if we are to be open to possibility, if we are to provide our creativity room to exercise.

Take a minute to dream right now. If you could imagine the ideal ensemble, what would it be? Be specific. Don't just say "A really great band." How would this ensemble *sound*? What repertoire would you perform? What would rehearsal be like? How much responsibility would the individual musician have? What kind of relationship would you have with the ensemble? Would you laugh more, share more personal musical experiences? Maybe you would like a more formal atmosphere, more structure than you have now. What kinds of performances would you do with this ideal ensemble and where would they be? Are there special areas of expertise or interest you would share? Most importantly, given your ideal ensemble, *what would you be free to do that you feel you can't do now?*

What is now just a creation in your mind has the potential to become reality. It doesn't matter how far away you are from this ideal, how many obstacles you face or how many other people think you are crazy. What *does* matter is that you have a dream that you believe in and that you keep that dream in front of you and take action on that dream. This fuels the vision you have for yourself and the organization and it is your privilege and responsibility to lead the way so it can become reality.

> Not much happens without a dream. And for something great to happen, there must be a great dream. Behind every great achievement is a dreamer of great dreams. Much more than a dreamer is required to bring it to reality; but the dream must be there first.[22]

FROM DREAM TO REALITY

Bringing that dream to reality requires that you take action. The problem with some visionaries is that they remain at the dream level and never take the steps needed to move the dream forward. As leaders we are compelled to act. A great dream without action is just a dream; if you don't move you can't lead. Leaders study the profession, set goals, take risks and reevaluate regularly. Leaders also know that moving from dream to reality means they must get to know and believe in the people they work with, depend and act on their foresight and they must remain passionate about their dream.

KEYS TO VISION
STUDY THE PROFESSION

We must be aware of what the profession as a whole is doing in order to create an organization that is alive and moving forward. No organization exists in a vacuum outside of the cultures in which it exists. Even *avant garde* ensembles are established against a backdrop of the norm. Knowing what other ensembles and organizations are doing is important not because we need to compete or keep up but because this knowledge helps provide a context for our work and our vision. It may help us to move in new directions or inspire us to

---

22   Greenleaf, 1977, 16.

take risks in repertoire or programming formats. More importantly, knowing what the wider profession is doing may provide insight into creating a unique niche for our ensemble, that is, answering a professional need that others haven't. Sometimes our organization is at a critical point, struggling with declining enrollment, audiences or shrinking budgets; at these times even more than others studying what we do and how we do it in light of the rest of the profession is a critical part of our leadership. In his study of companies that made the leap from good to great, Jim Collins found the ability to confront the brutal facts to be a hallmark of those who had been successful in making the leap:

> There is nothing wrong with pursuing a vision for greatness. After all, the good-to-great companies also set out to create greatness. But, unlike the comparison companies, the good-to-great companies continually refined the *path* to greatness with the brutal facts of reality.[23]

When we look at the profession we get an overview of the trends in performance, specifically the types of repertoire other ensembles are studying and the kinds of concerts they are giving. Exploring new repertoire is one of the easiest and most important ways to keep an ensemble alive and moving forward. Whether it is a new composition or a standard work we haven't yet experienced, repertoire that is new to us and to our ensemble presents musical and sometimes programming challenges that demand our collective growth. If we are consciously planning to move in a new direction, repertoire is a big part of that move.

---

23   *Good to Great* (New York: Harper Collins Publishers, Inc., 2001), 71.

When we study the profession we get ideas about programming and designing concerts. I remember the first time I came across a "prism" or "collage" concert. This is a joint performance by multiple ensembles within a school where each ensemble alternates presenting music from various locations within the hall or auditorium in a seamless fashion. An exciting event for audience and performers alike, it is a kind of concert that demands detailed planning and direction to pull off. Seeing this or any kind of performance first hand, such as demonstration concerts, lecture concerts, collaborative festivals, multi-media performances or audience participation concerts gets the visionary wheels turning and encourages us to think about our own programming and concert design in new and creative ways.

Studying the profession also gives us the opportunity to explore trends in thinking about the art form itself specifically as it relates to the kind of organization we lead. Whether we are learning about new teaching standards as a public school music educator or conduct in church, community or professional organizations, there are always new ideas about the role we play as leaders of the enterprise—about what we should be addressing in rehearsal, how rehearsals should be led, the relationship we have with the congregation or audience—that impact our vision for the organization.

Studying the profession can be a springboard for our thinking about where to go with our organization, acting as a catalyst for ideas and clarifying our thinking about the direction we need to take. Fortunately, as musicians we have many opportunities to do this kind of study. There are always conventions, workshops and concerts we can attend and professional journals and books we can read. The challenge is actually doing it, resisting the temptation to quarantine ourselves in our own building under the excuse that we don't have time or can't afford to leave to attend other events that might help enhance our vision and give it some practical direction. Conductors benefit by being in a community of musicians; every ensemble benefits when their leader is informed about the bigger professional picture.

Set Goals and Develop a Plan to Achieve Them

With a dream in place and knowledge of the wider profession providing a context we are ready to set goals and take action. Setting goals is a critical part of being a leader. Goal setting is a demonstration of our vision and a blueprint for action; goals give us a direction for the day, the week, the year—a reason to get out of bed each morning. Without goals we wander, procrastinate, and find ourselves stuck in the land of status quo.

Goals provide energy for conductors and ensembles. Everyone can get behind a goal that generates excitement, presents a challenge and demands something new. Whether it is tackling a different kind of repertoire, expanding the size of the ensemble or having more absence-free rehearsals, a goal can help bring us forward in the direction of our dreams.

Much has been written about the goal setting process. Personally I have been through extensive goal-setting exercises but I have found that the more elaborate the process, the less I focus on the actual goals. The last thing we need is another set of failed New Year's resolutions to make us feel guilty. You may find that having a few, strong, clearly articulated goals that you are absolutely passionate about is much more effective than a long list.

To determine your goals you need to have some time to reflect and a place where you can think uninterrupted. It may be your patio, a library or even a bustling coffee shop, as long as you can stay focused on the task. Start by writing down whatever goals come to mind. Don't edit or judge along the way; just write. Once you have a list, spend some time noticing which goals jump out at you, which ones you really feel strongly about. When I say strongly I don't necessarily mean the ones you feel most guilty about. The goals that speak to your heart, the ones that really move you and excite you, are the ones you want to pull out of the scribblings you made. It is those top two or three compelling goals on which you should focus.

Once you determine your top three goals, write them down and be sure to keep them with you (in a calendar, PDA or journal) so you can regularly revisit them. Ideally, devise some kind of timeline and action steps for each of your goals; without these, goals are just ideas with little hope of becoming reality. Regularly check your progress and readjust the timeline or action steps to accommodate your changing vision or unexpected events. Tell at least a few others—trusted colleagues, family, or friends—about these goals so they can hold you accountable. It is a lot easier to let goals slide if no one is around to ask you about them.

You don't necessarily need lofty, Miss America goals. If you are a young conductor or in a new position, your top goal may be non-musical in nature, such as "teaching the ensemble to stop immediately upon my release and to listen and wait for my comments without playing/singing or talking." This sounds so basic, but I have seen enough rehearsals during my student teaching supervising years to know that this very annoyance plagues most young (and many seasoned) conductors. You certainly can't lead a very productive and enjoyable rehearsal if every time you stop you have to wait, bang on the podium, lecture or talk over the ensemble to get their attention. Why not make this one of your top goals and develop action steps to be sure you can reach it?

Alongside practical goals will be other, more musical, creative goals. You may have goals related to musical independence (memorizing music, musicians making more creative decisions or smaller ensembles with fewer musicians on a part) or certain kinds of skills such as sight-reading or intonation. I caution against setting goals that are governed by other people's actions such as winning awards or coveted performance invitations. You can't control other people's actions or decisions, so focus on what you are in control of. For example, rather than winning an award at contest, make your goal for the ensemble "a musically expressive performance preceded by engaging rehearsals"; then you can devise a plan to achieve this goal. This keeps you centered on what is really important and does not negate the entire experience if the contest judge that day decided he preferred the orchestra with the pretty blue dresses over yours. (It happens.)

Goals will only work for your organization if you take the time to select them wisely and plan for their achievement. With each set of accomplishments you can set new goals and continue to move closer to your dream.

BE WILLING TO TAKE RISKS

The very nature of goals is that they push you to do something you haven't done before or bring you to a higher level. This involves risk taking, an essential characteristic of leadership. In most aspects of life I don't consider myself a risk taker. I'm not into death-defying sports, gambling at the local riverboat casino or even leaving the house without an umbrella on a cloudy day. I am, however, a risk taker when it comes to artistic endeavors, especially as a conductor. I have developed this ability by extending myself and challenging my ensembles to step out and try new things, knowing that they might not work (but always believing they will).

Playing it safe musically means staying at a level of repertoire that is easily achievable and therefore not likely to grow the ensemble as a group or as individuals. Playing it safe means predictable rehearsals and concerts which can lead to apathy and eventually a decline in attendance. Playing it safe means getting flabby, artistically speaking: letting our minds, our instruments and our musical soul atrophy.

Every conductor who considers herself a leader is at least in some respects a risk taker. When we revisit our vision for the organization we need to ask ourselves how we can extend ourselves to the next level. Even if the personnel in our ensemble change yearly, there are still ways to challenge our fledgling musicians and ourselves personally to reach a new level of excellence.

When musicians walk in the door for the first time they step into a legacy you and your previous ensembles have created. You may need to teach basic skills to these new musicians, but if you are a risk taker you will teach them in new ways and raise your expectations for what they can accomplish. You will continue to look at fresh ways of presenting your concert performances and look for higher quality, more interesting and more challenging repertoire. As I look through the concert programs of any ensemble I directed for several years, I always see a growth toward more challenging repertoire, more pieces that are out of the box in some way and even longer programs—meaning I challenged the ensemble and myself to prepare more music in the same amount of time without losing the quality of performance. Over time I designed different kinds of concerts, planned collaborations with other ensembles and utilized unique staging ideas. Ensembles always have turnover—musicians leave and new, often inexperienced musicians join—but as an *organization*, you can always move forward. Don't get caught up in thinking that because personnel change yearly you can never really move the organization forward; that you must always start at the *same beginning* as the year before. This mindset keeps organizations stuck at a very basic level and fosters a business-as-usual approach that can deaden the musical experience and short-change the musical product.

> Leaders are pioneers—people who are willing to step out into the unknown. They search for opportunities to innovate, grow, and improve…. Leaders know well that innovation and change all involve experimentation, risk, and failure. They proceed anyway. One way of dealing with the potential risks and failures of experimentation is to approach change through incremental steps and small wins. Little victories, when piled on top of each other, build confidence that even the biggest

challenges can be met. In so doing, they strengthen commitment to the long-term future.[24]

Take risks in your musical life as a conductor and leader. Try something new: research it, plan it and reevaluate as you go along, but don't stay in the safe zone or you will never move closer to your dream and the vision you have for the ensemble.

REEVALUATE REGULARLY

Leaders constantly move back and forth between vision (what they would like to see in the future) and reality (what is happening now). They have a goal and take action to move toward that goal, all the while assessing what is actually right in front of them. This commitment to regularly reevaluating progress is critical to our leadership ability and necessary when determining the next step. Reevaluating goals and the means of achieving them keeps the ensemble moving steadily forward and helps us determine an alternative plan when it is necessary.

For the conductor regular reevaluation happens on two levels. The first, broad level is in reevaluating our long-term goals as an organization, goals having to do with ensemble or audience growth, revenue, organizational structure or the overall artistry level and accomplishments of the ensemble. Generally speaking this kind of reevaluation is usually easier to plan for and carry out because it often feels natural to take stock at the end of the season on big issues such as these.

The other kind of reevaluating happens on a daily basis and usually applies to the ongoing progress of the ensemble toward the next performance. This regular, daily awareness of how things are going has direct impact not only on the ultimate performance but

---

24   Kouzes and Posner, 17.

also on the quality of the rehearsals that lead to that performance as well as the development and morale of the individuals in our ensembles. This kind of reevaluating is best accomplished by looking not at goals but by looking directly at those we lead:

> The measure of leadership is not the quality of the head, but the tone of the body. The signs of outstanding leadership appear primarily among the followers. Are the followers reaching their potential? Are they learning? Serving? Do they achieve the required results? Do they change with grace? Manage conflict?[25]

For conductors regular reevaluation means having an aural model in mind for the ensemble and the piece, devising rehearsal techniques and teaching methods to help the ensemble come closer and closer to that sound and committing to consistently and honestly reflecting on *what* the ensemble is producing and *how* they are working. If you have ever found yourself a few rehearsals away from a performance cramming music to get it learned in time, it may be that you didn't evaluate your progress carefully enough to adjust your plans in some way and avoid this last minute push. Maybe you over-programmed, leaving too little time to adequately study and prepare the music. Perhaps you overestimated the musicians' ability and chose repertoire that was not a good fit for their current level of ability. Or you might have selected a piece that demanded more of you as a teacher than you anticipated and found yourself at a loss as to how to bring the ensemble and the music together. Sometimes we under-program and find ourselves with an ensemble that is so bored with the music that they actually get worse every time they rehearse it. (This is a painful realization when it

---

25   Max De Pree, "What is Leadership?" in *Business Leadership: A Jossey-Bass Reader* by James M. Kouzes and Jossey-Bass Management Series, 65–6.

hits.) The point is, in each case we could have avoided these crisis situations if we had reevaluated regularly, considered our options and went to Plan B.

Plan B is any adjustment you make to the original plan. It may mean dropping a piece from the concert to allow for more rehearsal time on the other repertoire, using solos or a select ensemble to perform in place of the full ensemble, scheduling sectionals or bringing in recordings or guest artists to demonstrate and help teach an unfamiliar style. Whatever Plan B represents for you, the important thing is that you have one and that you *put it into place early enough for it to make a difference in the performance and the rehearsals*. Waiting until the dress rehearsal to pull a piece from the program is not only inefficient (think of all the time you spent working on it that could have been used on other things) but can also be demoralizing, leaving the ensemble with a sense of failure, frustration and wasted effort in the key rehearsals before a concert.

Reevaluation is a practice all good leaders engage in regularly. It helps ensure progress, protects process and keeps us on track toward product. Develop the discipline of regular reevaluation and have a Plan B ready to use if the need arises.

KNOW AND BELIEVE IN THE PEOPLE YOU LEAD

All that has been said so far about vision is dependent upon your desire to know and believe in the people you lead. As conductors we need to have a strong sense of intuition about people, especially the musicians in our ensemble. As we plan rehearsals or seasons, choose repertoire and design concerts and develop techniques and set goals we need to ask ourselves questions about the people we lead: What do they need now? How much can they absorb? When in the rehearsal period will they need recharging? When will they be most or least likely to be challenged? When will they need to be peaked? What speaks to them? What tires them? What motivates them? What do they want from this experience?

Conductors who are exemplary leaders and not just talented artists have a very special relationship with their ensemble, a relationship that is built on knowing the heart of the group as well as its individuals. Chapter III is devoted to the development of this relationship, but for now it is important to understand that without knowing and believing in the members of the ensemble it is virtually impossible to cast a vision for the future. Knowing the ensemble means learning who they are, what they are capable of and how they think and feel. This admittedly is a great challenge for young conductors or those in new positions. Even for seasoned conductors working with the same organization over a number of years this kind of people knowledge represents an ever-changing landscape but one which we can learn from if we choose to. Our efforts to get to know our ensemble will never be wasted.

Beyond knowing the ensemble we must believe in them and be very vocal about our confidence in their abilities. Whether you are conducting the children's choir at church or a professional orchestra, you must consistently let them know they are capable of even more than they imagine and tell them in such a way that motivates, not discourages or criticizes. If we don't believe in our ensemble we are not likely to take musical risks or set worthy goals. Believe in them and in your ability to bring out the best in them.

UTILIZE FORESIGHT

More than any other, foresight is that characteristic in a conductor that marks him as a true leader. Greenleaf called foresight the "central ethic of leadership" and described it this way:

> The leader needs two intellectual abilities that are usually not formally assessed in an academic way: he needs to have *a sense for the unknowable* and be able to

> *foresee the unforeseeable.* Leaders know some things and
> foresee some things which those they are presuming
> to lead do not know or foresee as clearly.[26]

Foresight and vision are closely related, as they both refer to the
ability to look ahead. Foresight, however, is the responsible, checks
and balances half of vision because it involves seeing the obstacles or
challenges that might be in the way of achieving a goal as well as the
strategies needed to avoid or overcome these obstacles. Foresight
is vision with wisdom. It is more than having an end goal; it is the
ability to also see how things will unfold on the way to the goal.

Foresight demands that we have insight into people and process,
into the art form at a creative (as well as a technical) level and that we
have a keen sense of time. Foresight instructs pedagogy. Pedagogy
helps us when a challenge arises but foresight tells us the challenge
is coming. Relying on foresight means we can plan ahead to create
the best possible product because we can see in advance what is
likely to happen with the process.

Vision is end-directed; foresight is means-sensitive. People
with foresight see multiple scenarios on the way to their visionary
goal and then determine a path that will hopefully bring the most
desirable scenario into reality.

For conductors foresight occurs on many levels. You may
have an overall vision for the organization in mind but can you *foresee*
the challenges or needs that lie ahead as you strive to accomplish
that vision?

You might envision a great concert or rehearsal but can you
see what it will take to get there? When we plan the concert season
foresight helps us see how programs fit together, how pieces flow
from one to the next, how the ensemble will grow because of the
repertoire and how the audiences will respond to the performances.
Foresight guides our rehearsal planning because we must rely on

---

26 Greenleaf, 1977, 21–22.

foresight to tell us before the actual rehearsal what problems the musicians will have and how we can rehearse in order that these challenges can be overcome.

Foresight becomes a barometer throughout the planning process as we encounter in our mind's eyes problems or barriers that we might face and then *change course accordingly*. It is foresight that helps us develop our Plan B even before it is needed.

Foresight demands that we use our intuition purposefully, regularly. Foresight is not some magic power but rather the use of our intuitive abilities and our experience to make good estimates of how the future may unfold. It employs our perceptive abilities in a different but equally important way as when we use them as artists perceiving musical possibilities.

Ultimately, foresight demands action if we are to be ethical in our leadership role. If we choose not to exercise our foresight we can be headed towards serious problems down the road, *problems that could have been avoided had we assumed our leadership responsibility and acted in advance*.

> The failure (or refusal) of a leader to foresee may be viewed as an *ethical* failure, because a serious ethical compromise today...is sometimes the result of a failure to make the effort at an earlier date to foresee today's events and take the right actions when there was freedom for initiative to act.[27]

A lack of foresight can result in a crisis and a recurrent lack of foresight usually means a recurrent crisis. While any organization can find a crisis on its hands, one that occurs with regularity means the leader has not utilized his foresight to determine the future course of events and take some action to avoid the crisis. "A recurrent crisis should always have been foreseen" says management expert

---

27   Greenleaf, 1977, 26.

Peter Drucker. "The recurrent crisis is simply a symptom of slovenliness and laziness."[28] If we find ourselves in the same problem situation for each concert or each season we have failed to use our foresight in ways that create positive change.

Can you develop foresight or is it something you either have or you don't? While foresight is likely a trait that occurs naturally in degrees within each one of us, it is a trait that can and must be sharpened. First simply become aware that foresight is a critical component of your leadership. Realize that foresight is the context for developing new techniques or strategies, a new structure for the organization or a more appealing marketing campaign. Too often we busy ourselves with the activities of being a conductor without a clear sense of how these activities interconnect and where they lead. Accepting the principle of foresight and its critical role in your leadership is the first step toward developing a stronger sense of it.

Secondly you must consciously practice using your foresight in your conducting life. Resist the temptation to work on impulse, especially when it comes to planning performances. Discipline yourself to set aside time so you can plan farther ahead, allowing yourself the opportunity to visualize and sketch out the rehearsal process. Take your score study and research to a different level in order to better anticipate the challenges that may arise. Practice the art of visualization as it relates to the logistics as well as the aesthetic flow of your performances. Think like the musicians in your ensemble when it comes to decisions impacting their experience and head problems off before they actually happen. These practices of foresight can greatly enhance every aspect of our leadership and every aspect of the ensemble's experience; a keener sense of foresight will ensure a stronger end result and a more edifying means of getting there.

---

28   Peter F. Drucker, *The Essential Drucker* (New York: Harper Collins, 2001), 237.

LET YOUR PASSION FUEL YOU

The final aspect of vision is the fuel for everything we do: our passion for music, for people, for performing and for life.

Passion plays an important role in creating and maintaining vision for the ensemble. Passion provides energy and direction. Passion gives us a reason to plan, to dream and to set high expectations. Passion keeps us moving forward even when challenges set us back. When we get overwhelmed by administrative details, by technical challenges and skill-development activities and by fund-raisers and audience-builders, it is our passion for music that brings us back to center and reminds us at a "feelingful" gut level *why* we are doing what we do.

Your passion for music is probably what drew you to conducting in the first place. An education department colleague of mine once remarked, quite disapprovingly, how our music students were the only ones in his class who routinely said they probably would *not* teach if they couldn't teach their chosen subject. While he viewed this as a lack of their passion for teaching, I saw it as a testimony to their very real passion for *music*. Typically conductors say that as they were growing up they loved being immersed in music so much that they had to find a way to be immersed for the rest of their lives. We want to share our passion for music with others and find we can do that by conducting an ensemble, creating music with other musicians and sharing it with audiences.

Passion keeps us open to the possibility that there is something out there we still don't know or haven't experienced. It keeps us in a learning, listening and loving frame of mind. If you lose the passion from your conducting life you will lose the very *reason* for vision. If you don't care, why should your ensemble or your audience? It will be too easy to go on automatic pilot and just keep replaying the same old record over and over. No passion, no vision.

41

THE VISION PAYOFF

Vision is essential to our success as leaders. The promise and the challenge are, I believe, as Peter Block described: "We live into the future that we imagine, and the task is to keep focused on that vision and let that be the context for all our actions."[29]

Taking the time to create and act upon a vision for your ensemble pays off in very real ways:

Vision provides energy, purpose, and direction for us as conductors. When we have a vision for what's next we automatically begin to move forward. We work with an energy that keeps us interest-*ing* because we are learning, curious and growing. It also keeps us interest-*ed* in others because we want to know what they have to say, what we can learn from them, and what needs they have that we can better meet. Deep in our core we feel a sense of purpose without which every day would be an endless set of tasks with no point. Vision is critical if we are to fully enjoy our lives.

Vision provides energy, purpose, and direction for the ensemble. Whether or not they say it, you can be sure the musicians will ask themselves from time to time "Why are we doing this? What is the point? Who cares what we do? Why should I attend rehearsal?" and other questions about their role or their significance. If the ensemble has a clear sense of direction and purpose—of vision— those questions can be answered internally. When the crunch times hit the musicians will have their own reservoir from which to draw strength: a reservoir that we continually fill by sharing our vision with them and by providing opportunities for them to contribute to and shape that vision.

Vision helps us avoid the avoidable. When we take the time to think through the logistics of programming, concert flow, rehearsals, special events or any of the many procedures we are responsible for we will envision problems or challenges. Fortunately they are

---

29   Peter Block, *The Answer to How is "Yes"* (San Francisco: Berrett-Koehler Publishers, Inc., 2002), 8.

problems only in our mind's eye at this point; we have the time to re-group and make changes that can help us avoid the avoidable and have a smooth event.

Vision keeps us organizationally efficient. When we think ahead we are more organized. We plan our time and that of the ensemble to be used efficiently, which everyone appreciates. When we make the effort to handle the administrative details by planning ahead we create trust with those who depend on us—our ensemble, our staff, our bosses, supervisors or board of directors. When we are efficient people feel cared for and that translates into stronger relationships.

In *On Becoming a Leader*, Warren Bennis identifies vision as the one characteristic common to every one of the leaders he studied. He writes:

> All leaders have the capacity to create a compelling vision, one that takes people to a new place, and then to translate that vision into reality. Not every leader I spoke with had all ten of the characteristics I am about to describe, but they all had this one. Peter Drucker said that the first task of the leader is to define the mission. Max DePree, in *Leadership Is an Art*, wrote, "The first responsibility of a leader is to define reality. The last is to say thank you. In between, the leader is a servant."[30]

VISION, FRUSTRATION, AND LONELINESS

The quote by John Adams at the beginning of this chapter is from what I find the most powerful moment in the musical *1776*: the point at which John Adams, whose conviction and vision made him

---

30   Bennis, 192.

a driving force behind the Declaration of Independence, becomes so frustrated at the unwillingness or inability of his fellow statesmen to see the promise of a free America that he becomes aware that he is alone. Adams was the quintessential visionary, able to see great potential despite dismal odds. Of course, it is easy to look back from our place in history and see the inevitability of the Declaration; but at the time Adams was fighting for this cause the end was not nearly as certain.

As conductors we can find ourselves in situations that feel just as frustrating, even if not as historically significant. The greater our ability to see potential the more likely we will feel alone. Operating from a framework of leadership rather than simply management means we have chosen to step out and define important values and believe in possibility, to select what is most important regardless of what others "know" is more practical or achievable:

> Acting on what matters means that we will consistently find ourselves feeling like we are living on the margin of our institutions and our culture. This calls for some detachment from the mainstream. It means we have committed ourselves to a state of eyes-open innocence designed to change the world we have inherited.[31]

We all operate within a larger framework: a school system, a church, a non-profit or professional organization. We have principals, booster boards, department chairs, deans, pastors and boards of directors, all of whom have something to say about the long-term welfare of the ensemble we direct. We may have been hired to fulfill a specific mission as laid out by one of these bodies and so are ethically and contractually obliged to meet this challenge.

---

31   Block, 84.

But our vision for the ensemble may be completely different from that of others in the organization because we know that our foresight and our ability to dream and use our teaching, conducting and administrative skills can make a higher level of artistry (or greater revenues, or larger audiences) a reality.

Even if we are given a specific goal or mission when we are hired, it does not mean that there is only one way to fulfill this mission; nor does it mean, with all respect, that those who hired us really know the ultimate potential of the ensemble and the wider organization. Without our passion, insight or experience, they cannot be expected to see what we see. Remember this: *Whether or not it was in the job description, providing vision—and selling that vision—are critical parts of our leadership lives.* We bring a kind of expertise to the job that no one else in the organization has; we must learn to use that expertise to accomplish what we are charged to do while at the same time provide a path for growth that will bring the ensemble to a place not even imagined by those who hired us. Our unique vision, built on our dreams and fueled by our imagination, is responsible for the approach we take to achieving the goals given to us and for the overall direction of the program even after those initial goals have been accomplished. Those who hired us, who provided the initial mission, will eventually look to us for direction; we must be ready to offer it.

There is always room for your unique contribution: your ideas, your imagination and your strategizing savvy in any musical organization. If that weren't the case then it would make little difference who stood on the podium. Vision is possibility, opportunity; *your* vision is your unique opportunity to contribute, to add value to others in a way that makes a difference. There is only one you. Begin dreaming—and dream big. You may feel lonely now but eventually your vision will be celebrated by many who couldn't even imagine what you knew was possible.

LITTLE SCHOOL, BIG VISION ～

Vision can seem like a blessing or a curse. When I chose to leave a secure position at a large regional university to rebuild a program at a small liberal arts college, most every colleague I knew warned me against it. Why leave an established program with beautiful facilities, an excellent faculty and plenty of opportunity for growth? What could I possibly gain?

Well, my colleagues couldn't see what I saw. I saw time: time with my daughter who was then just an infant, because making this change would mean I would be two miles from home instead of forty-five. The shorter commute combined with a less active, less visible and much smaller seedling program would give me more freedom to be a mom.

I saw opportunity: the opportunity to build a program that would combine the best of what large universities and small colleges could offer, and in doing so create a unique experience and quality of education that could be of great service to a varied population of students. And I trusted that if I made this decision based on principles and values that it would at the very least not send me spiraling backwards into a professional black hole.

As I write this it has been little more than a decade since I made that decision and I cannot begin to recount the blessings that have been bestowed on me in every way. The program at North Central College has grown to seventy music majors with 200 musicians actively involved in more than fifteen ensembles. We have trained many wonderful music educators, performers and conductors who are enjoying their own successes and we are currently in the process of developing a multi-venue arts district on campus to meet the needs of all our burgeoning arts programs. I have had many professional opportunities and acknowledgments, including being named the first recipient of an endowed chair in the fine arts, but best of all I have been able to be the very "present" parent I had envisioned some years ago. While life has not always been smooth or easy, it has always been right according to my values and vision. And it doesn't matter if others did not share my vision, though at times it can be maddening, frustrating and lonely.

Vision is one of your gifts and responsibilities as a conductor. Develop it and tap into it as a guide for your work and your life.

CHAPTER THREE

LEAD UPON TRUST ∿

Rhetoric and good intentions aside, if there is little or no
trust, there is no foundation for permanent success.
— Stephen Covey[32]

You have just accepted a new position, perhaps as conductor of choral activities for a large university or high school, artistic director of an area youth symphony or conductor of the local community band. You no doubt have a long list of responsibilities and directives from those who hired you as well as a wish list of your own as it relates to this new job. The ensembles you will be conducting may be accomplished and experienced or they may be struggling, artistically or otherwise, to keep their head above water. But while the specifics of each position will vary greatly, the primary need as you begin any new position is the same: to establish a trust relationship with the ensemble and other key figures in your organization.

Every relationship, in order for it to be successful and enduring, must be built on trust. We usually understand this principle as it relates to our personal lives, but how many of us have thought about the role that trust plays in our relationship with our ensembles? What constitutes trust between conductor and ensemble? How is it achieved? What benefits are gained from a two-way, trust relationship?

---

32   Stephen R. Covey, *Principle-Centered Leadership* (New York: Fireside, 1992), 17.

TRUST AND CHANGE

If there is one thing I wish I had understood as a new conductor it is the importance of developing trust relationships with the ensemble before attempting to institute significant change. As with many aspects of leadership, I had to learn it the hard way.

Like most conductors, I had been trained to take charge, to establish authority right from the start. (Remember that old teacher adage "Don't smile until Thanksgiving.") This meant among other things showing that I was a capable, knowledgeable conductor and teacher and that I could administrate the program. So early in my career, as I began a new high school choral position I eagerly took hold of the reins and began making decisions (usually changes) on any number of issues.

One of these decisions had to do with the singing of the "Hallelujah Chorus" at the end of the annual holiday concert. The tradition at this school had been that all choir members freshman through senior would combine to sing together with the orchestra to close the performance. While I was familiar with this idea, having done something similar at my previous position, I truly believed that only the top choir should sing this finale; they were the most developed singers, more capable of handling the piece well and had earned the right by virtue of their age and experience to sing this piece. Despite complaints from the students, I decided this was the right thing to do and went ahead with what turned out to be a significant change in the musical culture of that school.

As you might expect, I received many phone calls from parents upset that their freshman daughter and senior son who had looked forward to this "for *years*" would never have the chance again to sing together on stage. They were upset that this major tradition was being tossed aside, that this new conductor (what did she know, anyway?) had the nerve to make this change.

At the time, I remember thinking "Hey, who's the expert here? This is a better choice, vocally as well as programmatically speaking.

Let's give the students something to look forward to, to strive for during their choral career. It's my program; I can change it. What's the big deal, anyway?"

Now, as I look back I ask the same question but with a very different perspective: what *was* the big deal? Why not let them all sing together? I see now how much wiser it would have been to let tradition continue at least for a year or so. I would have gained so much more in building relationships by honoring what was obviously a revered tradition to that community than I ever did by displaying my authority or my pedagogical expertise. The reality is nobody cared about either of those things, at least not until they knew me and trusted me to guide and lead them. Had I embraced their tradition and become a part of the culture instead of setting myself apart from them (accentuating my outsider status), I would have built better trust relationships with students, colleagues and parents that, ironically, would have paved the way for all kinds of new ideas down the road—even though it would have meant deferring my plans for a time. Instead I held firm and alienated a lot of people, making it even more difficult to enact the really important changes later on.

I have seen this same scenario in the lives of many young professionals. I can think of two young, talented conductors who found themselves out of jobs not because they couldn't handle the musical challenges or even the managerial tasks but because they did not understand the importance of developing relationships before changing the world. I am coming to think of this phenomenon as directly proportionate to one's innate talents and passion. The more you have, the harder it is to resist the impulse to steamroll over people, even if for all the best musical and programmatic reasons.

Remember the story of the tortoise and the hare? Despite what seemed to be a hopeless case the tortoise wound up winning the race with his slow and steady approach. I often use this story as a metaphor for the way we high-energy, passionate, task-oriented types attack (yes, attack) a new conducting position. Because of our personality and our vision we can become impatient for change and growth. We can blast off with a burst of energy only to short-circuit when we meet the most important challenge: developing trust relationships with people.

KEYS TO TRUST
EMBRACE THE TRUST PARADOX

Trust must precede change, at least significant change, if we are to be successful in the long run. Think of it this way: when we stand in front of an ensemble as their new conductor, their security is threatened. Even if they didn't like the previous director they at least knew what to expect and took comfort in that routine. Now, with a new leader all of their energy is focused on getting accustomed to us: our conducting technique, our rehearsal style, our manner of communicating ideas and our sense of humor (or lack of it). Asking them to get to know us and accept all new traditions and practices simultaneously means we have stripped them of their foundation altogether, making it very difficult for us to work together toward a mutual goal. Without a reasonable degree of security the ensemble will not be able to perform musically, to sing or play expressively. It is our job to be sure they can by accepting who they are and encouraging them to move forward with us.

But does this mean we have to put up with everything just as we found it? What if the ensemble lacks focus, discipline or if they are downright unruly? Do we just go with it? What if their repertoire diet is the equivalent of candy and soda or if their concert demeanor is unprofessional? Are we obligated to let them stay in their comfort zone? Maybe the organization's programming decisions are driving them further and further into debt. Do we wait to intercede?

This brings us to the other side of the trust paradox. Just as the members of the organization desire security, they *also expect that we will lead them forward, which means some things must change.*

While they may not be conscious of it or may not verbalize it, the musicians want to get better, move to the next level and be engaged and interested in rehearsal; even those in unruly ensembles desire, down deep, for someone to provide structure and direction so they don't have to walk into chaos every day. So while building trust depends in some measure on maintaining tradition, it also depends on making some changes early on that will provide a working framework for success.

The bottom line is we need to choose our battles. Assess the situation as you come into a new position. Decide what absolutely must be in place for you to lead a productive, engaging and musically satisfying rehearsal and what policies and procedures need to be in place for the organization to accomplish at least the very next goal facing you if not your ultimate goals. Let the rest go for now, even if it means you continue to do those marathon Pancake Breakfast performances (I remember those well), participate in a competitive marching program or continue to mount large masterworks when you really want to perform more contemporary repertoire. As you build trust, establish credibility and develop a history with the organization you can move in the direction of almost any change. In the meantime you will also learn some things from their history that may help you see things from a new perspective.

BE CONSISTENT TO BE TRUSTWORTHY

For us to gain trust we must be trustworthy. The simplest way to become trustworthy is to be *consistent*. When we are consistent in our daily actions, in our preparation and the manner in which we deal with people, we are viewed as worthy of trust. The musicians in our ensembles see our consistent selves as our authentic selves; every day they are learning who we really are and they gradually come to trust that person. When we are inconsistent—that is, different from day to day, rehearsal to rehearsal—musicians wonder "Who is this conductor, really? Which one is the real person and which is the image he wants us to believe?"

> To trust a leader, it is not necessary to like him. Nor is it necessary to agree with him. Trust is the conviction that the leader means what he says. It is a belief in something very old-fashioned, called "integrity." A leader's actions and a leader's professed beliefs must be congruent, or at least compatible. Effective leadership—and again this is very old wisdom—is not based on being clever; it is based primarily on being consistent.[33]

Being consistent is not an easy task for most passionate, artistic types. The fuel that drives our passion for music can also start a fire of impatience and sarcasm on the podium when things are not going well. What started with a jovial warm-up period can disintegrate into a heated, tense rehearsal if we are not careful to guard our trustworthiness. Stories of conductor tantrums are so much a part of our musician folklore that we have sadly come to take this kind of behavior for granted. We not only expect dramatic behavior from conductors, we sometimes almost encourage it, assuming it is a sign of great creative genius. And while it is easy to see how passion, creativity and tantrums go together, *dramatic, negative behavior is not only unnecessary, it is actually detrimental to an excellent artistic experience and product.* Why? Because playing or singing expressively depends on an openness of heart, something that only comes authentically when there is trust between conductor and ensemble. Any change in the ensemble's behavior or performance resulting from our explosion on the podium is short-lived; our temperamental behavior is a form of coercion and coercion never leads to positive relationships.

---

33   Drucker, 271.

CONNECT TO THE ENSEMBLE
—ONE MUSICIAN AT A TIME

"To connect to people in a group, relate to them as individuals."[34] Conductors deal with groups of people, sometimes very large groups. This can make it difficult to develop a trust relationship because there is little opportunity to connect with musicians on an individual level. However, it is important for conductors to make every attempt to do so, because connection builds trust.

> Some leaders have problems with the Law of Connection because they believe that connecting is the responsibility of followers. That is especially true of positional leaders. They often think, *I'm the boss [conductor]. I have the position. These are my employees [musicians]. Let them come to me.* But successful leaders who obey the Law of Connection are always initiators. They take the first step with others and then make the effort to continue building relationships. That's not always easy, but it's important to the success of the organization. A leader has to do it, no matter how many obstacles there might be.[35]

The time immediately before and after rehearsals is prime time to connect with musicians. While conductors usually want time prior to rehearsal to get focused and put the final touches on the rehearsal plan, using at least a few minutes when you enter the rehearsal room to talk with the musicians individually can prove invaluable in establishing a connection. Simply saying hello, asking how their day has been or commenting on the weather, the latest sports event in the news or some other item of mutual interest

---

34 John C. Maxwell, *The 21 Irrefutable Laws of Leadership*, 104.
35 Maxwell, 104.

establishes you as a real person, one who authentically cares about other people. Personally speaking, those minutes just before I start rehearsal with the Women's Chorale have come to be among the most enjoyable for me because we laugh, joke and commiserate about the busyness of life. This informal interaction is a de-stressor and in many ways keeps us from taking ourselves too seriously. More importantly, it always seems to lead to better concentration and a more productive rehearsal. Even in festival situations where I am working with as many as 400 singers I will use part of my break time to walk through the aisles and talk to as many individuals as I can. Even though I can't get to everyone, the entire group sees me making the effort and always responds with greater connection once the rehearsal resumes.

As you connect with the musicians you must be sure to be authentic in your dialogue or your attempts at becoming trustworthy will backfire. If they believe you are just going through the motions or are trying to manipulate them in any way they will resent your efforts and can become resistant in rehearsal. You also must avoid talking only to the same group of individuals, because this sends the message that there are a favored few. It may be helpful to focus on a different section of the ensemble each time, thereby ensuring that you will eventually cover them all.

Connecting to people as individuals has great relational benefits which directly translate to your working relationship as conductor and ensemble.

> When a leader has done the work to connect with his people, you can see it in the way the organization functions. Among employees [musicians] there are incredible loyalty and a strong work ethic. The vision of the leader becomes the aspiration of the people. The impact is incredible.[36]

---

36   Maxwell, 107.

LISTEN

Connecting to the members of your ensemble means listening to them. Sounds simple, but we can be so driven as conductors that we plow through rehearsals and plow over people without even realizing it. Sometimes just providing an opportunity for the musicians to be heard can go a long way toward developing a trust relationship.

There are many ways to listen to the members of the ensemble. In addition to connecting with them while they enter or leave rehearsal we can find interesting (but practical) ways for them to provide input into the creative process. In *The Art of Possibility*, Boston Philharmonic conductor Benjamin Zander talks about his use of "white sheets" as a way of connecting with and listening to his ensemble.

> With the intention of providing a conduit for orchestra members to be heard, I initiated a practice of putting a blank sheet of paper on every stand in each rehearsal. The players are invited to write down any observation or coaching for me that might enable me to empower them to play the music more beautifully. At first I braced myself for criticism, but surprisingly the responses on the "white sheets," as they have come to be called, rarely assume that form.[37]

You might find this practice inviting or positively frightening, depending on your personality and on your relationship to the ensemble. You may think this is impractical and indeed, in certain situations, such as large high school performing programs, it may

---

37   Rosamund Stone Zander and Benjamin Zander, *The Art of Possibility* (New York: Penquin Books, 2000), 70–71.

be. The point here is that as conductors who are determined to lead and not just dictate we need to provide opportunities for the musicians to have a voice, not only as a tool to building trust, but also as a way of improving everyone's level of creativity and artistry. Ask them for suggestions and listen, *really* listen to what they say. You might not take their suggestion but can learn something from the input they provide—and that in itself is worth the effort it takes on your part. And in many cases you might just find that their ideas about interpretation or intent are highly intuitive and on target; they might even see something you don't see.

> Frequently I receive comments that are deeply insightful about the interpretation, comments that I almost always take on board and that affect the performance. An orchestra of a hundred musicians will invariably contain great artists, some with an intimate or specialized knowledge of the work being performed, others with insight about the tempo or structure or relationships within the piece, a subject about which no one has ever asked them to communicate.[38]

Even if you do not work with a professional ensemble you will be surprised at the insight musicians have about the piece. After all, they are the ones playing it, fingering it, singing it and breathing it. Even the youngest or most inexperienced musicians using non-technical language can shed light on the music or the musical/technical process that can make a difference in how we learn, create, perform and lead.

---

38   Zander and Zander, 71.

Trust and Empower the Ensemble

Only empowered people can reach their potential. When a leader can't or won't empower others, he creates barriers within the organization that people cannot overcome. If the barriers remain long enough, then the people give up, or they move to another organization where they can maximize their potential.[39]

Listening is the first step toward empowering our musicians to be fully creative and invested in the process of music making. Empowering means "giving power to," something conductors generally do not do with their ensembles.

Not only do the musicians need to learn to trust us, we must be willing to trust the musicians. This means believing that they are capable of accomplishing a great deal, even more than they themselves believe. It also means understanding that they want more ownership of the creative process than we usually give them and trusting that they can make good decisions when given the opportunity to do so.

Trusting the ensemble means letting go of some of the control that we worked so hard to gain in the first place, and for most conductors that's a scary proposition. But by trusting we empower the musicians; we give them permission to be more fully involved in determining their experience and ultimately their success.

Leaders make it possible for others to do good work. They know that those who are expected to produce the results must feel a sense of personal power and ownership. Leaders understand that the command-and-control techniques of the Industrial Revolution

---

39   Maxwell, 126.

no longer apply. Instead, leaders work to make people feel strong, capable, and committed. Leaders enable others to act not by hoarding the power they have but by giving it away.... [W]hen people are trusted and have more discretion, more authority, and more information, they're much more likely to use their energies to produce extraordinary results.[40]

Empowerment will be a major thread throughout this book because it is the key to understanding leadership as an interactive process, one that focuses on growth and autonomy. Greenleaf said that the best test of the servant-leader is to ask:

Do those served grow as persons? Do they, *while being served,* become healthier, wiser, freer, more autonomous, more likely themselves to become servants?[41]

In Chapter IV we will look at how to structure a rehearsal which fosters empowerment and autonomy. For now, remember that empowerment means involving the musicians in decision making and putting some of the burden on them for the quality of their ensemble. Believe that they can do more than follow our instructions.

Truly, believing is seeing. We must, therefore, seek to believe in the unseen potential. This creates a *climate for growth and opportunity.* Self-centered people [conductors] believe that the key lies in them, in their techniques, in doing "their thing" to others. This works only temporarily. If you believe it's "in"

---

40   Kouzes and Posner, 18.
41   Greenleaf, 1977, 13–14.

them, not "in" you, you relax, accept, affirm, and let it happen. Either way it is a self-fulfilling prophecy. [42]

SET THE TONE FOR TRUST IN THE REHEARSAL

As the leader of the experience we are the ones primarily responsible for setting the tone or the atmosphere of the rehearsal. This means everything from establishing a sense of commitment or a work ethic to using our sense of humor in appropriate ways and at the right time.

If we approach rehearsal with anticipation (not anxiety) and are prepared in our rehearsal plan and score study we communicate through our actions that rehearsal time is important and will be used efficiently and purposefully. If we freely display our passion for music, eventually that passion will be contagious. The musicians will learn that they have permission to express themselves and that it's okay to "feel" the music. Yes, even junior high boys will respond to our passion for the music given time, lots of encouragement and the conductor's savvy in knowing how to deal with this age group.

A big part of setting the tone has to do with making mistakes. When we establish a working environment where ideas can be tested and evaluated, mistakes and failure take on an entirely different look. Mistakes are just part of the learning, checkpoints along the way to shaping the music, learning technical skills and developing musical understanding. Anyone can make a mistake (including conductors, remember), so we should be able to admit it and move on. Often I'll stop rehearsal to check out something I heard and before I can get very far a hand will shoot up: "Sorry, that was me; I've got it now." (Or in true college speak: "My bad—duh!") It never ceases to surprise and delight me that people will recognize and admit their own errors when they feel they are in a safe enough environment to do so. My response to that singer is always "Great!

---

42   Covey, 35.

Thanks." Similarly, when I miss a cue or find myself conducting in one because I lost my place in the score (you do it, too), I also can stop, admit it and get back in the game, so to speak, without feeling as though I have lost the respect of the ensemble. While trust is based on many things, it is not dependent on perfection.

Why do so many conductors feel it necessary to operate in an either/or mode when it comes to the working environment in the rehearsal? It is not only possible but also important to balance a sense of urgency and intense focus with a joy for what we do and an appreciation for those situations that are genuinely funny. Sometimes laughing provides just the release needed from several minutes of intense work and it can contribute to the camaraderie of the group. As long as we are not laughing at anyone's expense or using sarcasm in a cutting way, laughter is an important element in a successful rehearsal.

> If you—and others—aren't having fun doing what you're doing, chances are you're not doing your best. We aren't talking about a laugh-a-minute party, but the overall experience should be enjoyable. Appropriate humor can lead to cohesion and bonding among coworkers.[43]

BE HONEST

Setting a high bar for the ensemble demands that we provide feedback about how they are doing. And while we want to be encouraging and positive, we must be honest as well. Always telling them "great job" means there is no distinction between one behavior and another. The ensemble will come to distrust us because they know, even if they don't verbalize it, whether they hit the mark or not. If we don't recognize those missed marks and hold them

---

43   Kouzes and Posner, 198.

accountable we are sending a message that either we don't know enough to judge their work or we don't care enough to make it better. Neither message is one we want to send.

So how do we handle missing the mark: when the ensemble is not playing as well as they can, when the concert didn't quite "click" or when the choir receives a Division III at contest? How can we be honest without totally losing momentum, jeopardizing morale or shaking their faith in us as their conductor?

First, it is important that we honestly assess our role in missing the mark. Did we over-program for the concert and therefore leave too little time to prepare each piece adequately? Did we fail to design rehearsals that would lead to a thorough understanding of the music? Was there something we could have done better, something as simple as giving clearer instructions in rehearsal that would have helped avoid an unsuccessful situation? If so, we need to accept this and learn from it so that we do not continue to make the same mistakes. It is easy for us to put complete responsibility on our musicians without realizing that ultimately we are responsible for setting them up for success.

For example: we recognize that it is the musician's responsibility to practice. I cannot practice *for her*. If she wants to be an excellent musician and be a part of an excellent ensemble she must discipline herself to practice. *At the very same time*, if she does not practice I must also look inward at my actions. Did I make my expectations clear? Was I inconsistent in holding musicians accountable for their own practicing? Was I reasonable about the amount of time and music assigned for practice? Am I, *through the quality of the experience I craft*, providing the right incentive and understanding which would motivate a student to follow through on practice? These questions help me to be honest with myself as well as with the musicians.

When are we dishonest as conductors? When we fail to prepare for rehearsals or performances; when we blame judges or clinicians for their comments or ratings when there is truth in their judgments; when we blame our ensemble for these shortcomings when they

63

really are reflections of our own. We are dishonest when we regularly make poor use of rehearsal time and find ourselves force-feeding music to the ensemble just in time for a public performance.

Being honest with the ensemble means first being honest with ourselves and taking ownership for our mistakes. Once we do that we have a much more objective assessment of the situation and can authentically hold the ensemble accountable for their part of the deal. When we hold ourselves to high standards and admit it when we miss the mark, but also *go forward and learn from it*, musicians will be much more likely to follow suit. Our character comes through loud and clear in these situations, and when people see character growing right in front of them they tend to mature in their own growth.

Being honest with the ensemble also means redefining the notion of failure. Rather than viewing every missed mark as a negative, we can think of it as a learning opportunity—for the ensemble and for us.

> Failure is a subjective label we apply to unintended or unexpected experiences... It is life attempting to teach us some new lessons or trying to point some new directions.... The next time you are experiencing something you didn't intend or expect, ask yourself, "What am I supposed to be learning from this?" When we are living life on-purpose, every life experience helps us to solve the hieroglyphic of meaning.[44]

---

44 Cashman, 80.

TRUST AS A PRELUDE TO ARTISTIC ACHIEVEMENT

Ultimately, developing and maintaining a trust relationship between you and your ensemble paves the way for artistry. Think of all the things we ask of the musicians—things that lead to a fine artistic product—that demand their trust in us: developing and experimenting with their technique, whether it is the adolescent boy going through a voice change or trained adults learning to create non-traditional sounds on their instrument for an *avant garde* piece; playing and singing expressively, intimately and without fear of opening their souls to the listener; absorbing a great deal of music and detail in a two-hour rehearsal. Whatever it might be, we are always asking the ensemble to trust in our musical skill and knowledge, our planning ability, our intuition and our character by the things we ask of them. When this relationship is established we can all go much further in creating our art.

Similarly, when we trust that the musicians are capable of taking more ownership of the creative decision making process they feel more invested in the ensemble and something almost magical happens. Our experiences, both in rehearsal and performance become charged with what I call the X Factor. The X Factor is that special character, that magic that the musicians bring to the performance *when they see themselves as real contributors.* It is an emotional, physical and intellectual investment that goes beyond doing a good job. During a recent performance at our state music conference the Women's Chorale stunned audiences with an improvisatory piece which is performed without a conductor. Based on a Balinese ritual, this exciting piece uses a "caller" (one of the singers) to determine when to move the piece to the next section. The singers are staged in an unorthodox arrangement and each group has the responsibility for connecting visually and musically with its own members as well as with the other groups during this fast-paced, cathartic and highly charged piece.

Watching the performance off-stage was an incredible experience for me, not just because of the technical and musical energy displayed but because the X factor was in full force. Without a conductor and faced with a challenging and non-traditional piece the singers had to depend on their understanding (developed in rehearsal) and needed to trust themselves and each other to make decisions, in real time, that would lead to a successful performance. Regardless of the applause and congratulations that followed, these women knew they had done well because they were fully invested in the process and were able to recognize the synergy on that stage.

The X Factor makes a performance and even a rehearsal memorable. It is the result of mutual trust between and among the conductor and ensemble members and is the payoff from our conscious decision to allow the ensemble to be more active participants in the creative process. Even the most well rehearsed and technically proficient ensembles will lack something in their performance experience if they are not given this opportunity. I could never mandate what the X Factor brings to the music. Trust the ensemble. Be trustworthy in your actions and you will all reap the benefits for a long time to come.

ARE KIDS ARTISTS? ᴖ

Some of you work with children: maybe an elementary school chorus, a junior high band or a high school orchestra. You've just read about trust, empowerment and honesty and a lot of things that, frankly, you might be thinking can't apply to your situation. Your daily existence seems to be filled with keeping the group in line; just getting them follow the music, put their instruments together or watch you for a cue are major accomplishments.

Are kids artists? Are they capable of operating at a high level and can they be trusted to think analytically about what is happening in the music? Can they perform expressively and with real understanding?

Your answer to that question will determine how you will lead: what you will expect, what you will believe they can accomplish and the way you will choose your repertoire, design your rehearsals and program your season. Kids are not age-deficient humans; they are thinking, feeling (okay, maybe sometimes feeling too much), creating beings that can accomplish amazing things. When you provide them with the tools, the opportunity for excellence and encouragement along the way, they will surprise you with behaviors and attitudes that can justifiably be called artistic. Their ability to understand and process information at a high level will astound you.

When the Pokemon craze was at its height I was reminded of how much detail kids can handle. My daughter was in second grade at the time and could easily write out dozens and dozens of character names, along with all kinds of stats and characteristics that were included on the cards, from memory. Today kids of all ages have technological knowledge and keyboarding skills that far exceed even the most highly educated adults (ahem). And watch them on an electronic dance mat as they deftly follow a complicated set of arrows moving to the music at lightning speed. So why do we think that learning three scales—*maybe*—is all they can handle when they start playing their instruments? Why do students show up to their college auditions after four or six years (or more) of musical involvement and still struggle to identify the key of a piece? Why can't they pronounce the names of the composers they supposedly have studied for months or sing or play a beautifully arched phrase? Because we don't really believe they can and that belief governs the way we conduct, teach and lead these artists-in-waiting.

Trust your kids. They can do it if you teach them well. Trust yourself. You can find creative, effective ways to develop these young artists despite twenty-minute rehearsal periods, poor facilities or minimal budgets. Bottom line: when the rehearsal door is closed and there is no one around to applaud, it's you, your kids and a world of possibilities. Don't allow yourself to feel trapped by standards and assessment. Use them as a catalyst to find ways of reaching and teaching your kids. Don't get discouraged by lack of resources or complicated scheduling challenges. As you keep working on ways to change the situation, use your creativity to design learning opportunities in spite of the challenges. And if you are lucky enough to be in a setting that has all these things in place, be grateful, step up the level of the work you do and extend a hand to those colleagues who may not be quite so fortunate.

You are the door to your kids' artistry. Open up.

CHAPTER FOUR

LEAD BY TEACHING ~

Teachers possess the power to create conditions that can help students learn a great deal—or keep them from learning much at all.

—Parker Palmer[45]

Teaching from the podium is one of the most exciting and challenging aspects of the conductor's job. Even with the most experienced or professional ensembles, relaying information, interpreting musical intent, engaging musicians in the discovery of what the music has to offer and developing individual and ensemble skill and understanding all fall under the "teacher" part of the conductor's role. Every time we share an idea, every time we show in our gesture how to shape a phrase, every time we inform the ensemble about stylistic practice and context and every time we strive to inspire the musicians to achieve at the highest level possible, we are teaching. "One might argue that everything involved in rehearsing and conducting can be characterized via a teaching paradigm, even in a professional ensemble environment."[46]

But as conductors we often experience an internal conflict when it comes to thinking of ourselves as teachers. At a deep level we realize we're teachers, but in practice we don't want to admit it to

---

45   Parker J. Palmer, *The Courage to Teach* (San Francisco: Jossey-Bass Publishers, 1998), 6.
46   Richard Parncutt and Gary E. McPherson, ed., *The Science and Psychology of Music Performance* (New York: Oxford University Press, Inc., 2002), 336.

ourselves or to others. We go through a kind of unspoken identity crisis in our conductor lives. Instead of thinking of or referring to ourselves as teachers we prefer to be thought of as *artists*: creative, talented and unique professionals. We enjoy people's reactions when they ask what we do for a living and we say "I am a *conductor*." Once they realize we don't mean the railroad kind (it's just a few seconds, but there's always a pause), they often respond with a mix of awe, interest and respect, and even seem a little starstruck. No nine-to-five job for us, no cubicles, no same-old same-old. We are *exciting* people.

We know we spend much of our professional lives *teaching* but struggle with the reality that teachers are not always highly regarded. In the same way the word "servant" can have negative connotations depending on one's perspective, the word "teacher" can be thought of in a less-than-celebrated way. If you think of teaching as a noble profession, one of service and commitment (as indeed it can be), you have a positive viewpoint and are happy to be thought of as a teacher. But if you think of teaching as the job for someone who couldn't compete at a high enough level (you've bought into the misguided idea that "those who can, do; those who can't, teach"), then teaching is not a career you prefer to be associated with, at least not as your primary professional identity. Thinking of ourselves as teachers instead of as conductors means others might think less of our creativity and talent. We fear that we might not be seen as "the real deal," especially those of us who conduct within an academic setting because after all, if we were the real deal, why would we be *teaching*?

This internal struggle does more than dictate what we put on our business card. The way we think of ourselves and define our jobs in our own mind has everything to do with the way we execute our jobs and with the way we lead. If we think of ourselves at least in part as *teachers* when we are on the podium we will have a distinctive way of sharing information and relating with the ensemble. If for whatever reason we do not think of teaching as fundamental to what we do, our approach will be different in style, content and philosophy.

Conductors who lead from the podium do so by showing the ensemble where to "go," musically and expressively speaking. They *teach*—through their words, their gesture, their passion and their pedagogy—and they plan and prepare for these experiences to happen efficiently and meaningfully. The best leaders embrace the teaching part of their role and welcome the opportunity to develop the skill and understanding of the musicians they lead. They spend a significant amount of their preparation time devising teaching strategies and work to find ways to involve the musicians in the learning process so that they become engaged and ultimately, empowered to make creative decisions collaboratively and independently as mature artists. And they don't apologize for the teaching that they do.

This chapter is all about the teaching part of the conductor-leader's job: about finding a way of leading through teaching that develops the ensemble and the individual musicians to become more than good at following directions. It is about shaping the experience by the work we do outside of rehearsal as well as on the podium and about shaping the musicians to help them move to the next level whatever their age, experience or professional status. It is about moving from being a good conductor to being a great conductor by the quality of the teaching that we do.

LIMITING BELIEFS ABOUT THE TEACHING CONDUCTOR

Before we can talk about great teaching we need to recognize that we and our musicians hold some limiting beliefs about the nature of ensemble music-making that can get in the way of teaching for our best experience and performance.

From the conductor's perspective, first is the limiting belief that "I don't have enough time for teaching; I am too busy getting a concert ready." We rationalize that because we only meet once a week or because there's too much to be taught due to the wide

71

disparity in abilities and backgrounds we can't really do anything but prepare pieces for the next performance.

Time is a challenge in every ensemble setting and particularly so in community and church environments. Getting a full service ready in one rehearsal with amateur musicians and a fluctuating roster of singers can be overwhelming. But consider the fact that it is the *quality* of the time we spend with the ensemble that matters when it comes to being able to teach more than "how the parts go." We have a choice: we can, for example, either take ten minutes at the beginning of rehearsal to warm up by going through the same routine with minimal comments, instruction or expectations *or* we can use *the same ten minutes* to teach them something that will help develop a part of their musical selves. We don't need to *add* time to rehearsal to teach, but we *do* need to use the time in such a way that it is focused on growth rather than the minimum skill acquisition required to make it through the next performance. Peter Block believes "We have time for all that is truly important to us, so the question of time shifts to What is important? When we say something takes too long, it just means that it does not matter to us."[47] We need to change our perspective on our role and lead the way to a rich musical experience by improving the quality of the teaching we provide, even and maybe especially in challenging circumstances.

On the other side of the podium musicians often hold the limiting belief that once they "arrive" musically or professionally (wherever that is) they no longer need to be taught and they certainly don't want a conductor trying to teach them. Advanced musicians come to possess a self-sufficiency that may make them resistant to our attempts at teaching. This makes working with professional, semi-professional or even collegiate ensembles a challenging enterprise for any conductor.

---

47   Block, 34.

There is no question that mature musicians who have developed a high level of artistic skill and have amassed a good deal of experience do not need to be instructed in the same way that a beginner will. However, they still must be taught to use their talents *collectively* so that the ensemble (a group of individual opinion holders) can function as an artistic whole. Peter Drucker describes the challenge this way:

> Any business enterprise must build a true team and weld individual efforts into a common effort. Each member of the enterprise contributes something different, but they must all contribute toward a common goal. Their efforts must all pull in the same direction, and their contributions must fit together to produce a whole—without gaps, without friction, without unnecessary duplication of effort.[48]

We may not commonly refer to this welding process as teaching, preferring to call it leading, guiding, coaching, facilitating or just conducting, but if teaching can be defined as "bringing understanding to somebody, especially through an experience," then the conductor's way of helping musicians understand how to unify efforts as they perform is teaching in the clearest sense.

If you conduct an experienced ensemble you will likely encounter skeptical or even arrogant attitudes on the part of some of the musicians. This resistance can be overcome in time. Once the ensemble sees that you respect their talent and experience and are assured by your approach to the rehearsal that you are not going to talk down to them or treat them as less-than-capable musicians, they will come to trust you and open up to your ideas. Whether they realize it or not, they will become the benefactors of your teaching and will grow in ways even they had not imagined.

---

48   Drucker, 112.

Only when you banish these limiting beliefs from your psyche and help the musicians to do likewise can you move forward to developing a teaching approach from the podium that leads to engaging rehearsals and rewarding, high-quality performances.

KEYS TO TEACHING
BALANCE PROCESS WITH PRODUCT

As conductors we are charged with the responsibility of creating a product to be enjoyed in a public performance. We live our lives feeling pressed for time (if we only had another week...) and judged solely on our product: the quality and success of our most recent performance. The pressure to create something of high quality—something which will be respected, appreciated and maybe even regarded as highly artistic—can often drive us to ignore the means we use to get to this end: to focus on product at the expense of process.

A product focus usually leads to a one-way, conductor-centered rehearsal; with the product in mind, we start and stop the ensemble, diagnosing problems and prescribing solutions. To be sure, this is an efficient method of running a rehearsal and a pedagogical skill that must be mastered by all conductors. However, while it is a necessary skill, it is not sufficient if we are really interested in *maximizing the musical experience so that both product and the process that brings it into being are meaningful and creative*. A strictly diagnostic/prescriptive approach makes the ensemble completely dependent upon us and often means starting at square one when we finish one concert and begin preparing the next. Because they have not been part of the process of making musical decisions, or at the very least have not been privy to the rationale behind the musical decisions we make on their behalf, the musicians' growth is limited and almost completely tied to the challenges of their specific vocal or instrumental part. Their larger understanding and overall musical experience may be compromised because we have taken complete ownership of the process in our quest for the ultimate product. Meanwhile, the musicians have functioned as artisans instead of artists, doing what we tell them to do but only minimally creating while they do it.

> When performance group directors or classroom teachers are directing the music making of students but make all the decisions *for* them ("Trumpets, play those two measures louder," "Sing the beginning of the song with shorter notes," "Altos, you're getting that rhythm mixed up; do it like this," "Hold that trill longer, then fade out," and on and on forever), those *directors* are creating, but their students are surely not. The students have been forced to be artisans, used for making art but permitted no involvement in artistic creation.[49]

An imbalanced focus on product is the major roadblock we face as conductors. Clearly it is important to have an end goal to strive towards, but the process of getting to the goal—a complex, ever-changing, wonderful mix of experiences—must be considered and crafted just as carefully if the moments of rehearsal are to be rich, rewarding and full of potential—*and if the performance that results from these rehearsals is to be alive and insightful.*

While it happens less often, it is also possible to balance the process/product equation in the other direction: to focus so heavily on *process* that we forsake product in our teaching from the podium. This happens when we start believing that we must accept any quality of work from the musicians as long as they feel good about it, are happy and are having fun. Admittedly, great teachers value having fun and want their ensemble to have a high level of

---

49   Bennett Reimer, *A Philosophy of Music Education*, 2nd ed. (Englewood Cliffs, NJ: Prentice Hall, 1989), 69.

self esteem but it is unreasonable to expect that there will be no tough rehearsals, no need to challenge the ensemble out of their comfort zone or no struggles with the music. Being creative doesn't always feel good; indeed, it is precisely the struggle—the wrestling with artistic challenges and experimenting with various ways of tackling them—that gives meaning to the experience. Don't rob the ensemble of this creative *Sturm und Drang* because you are worried that they might get discouraged or will stop trying. Ask yourself and the ensemble: "If we have no product, no clear end goal to aim for, what are we working towards? What is the measure of our learning, of our development?" Just as with a product focus, we need to guard against an imbalance toward process if it weakens our eventual artistic outcome enough to make the experience seem pointless.

Process and product go hand in hand: you can't have one without the other, so at some level it is unrealistic to talk about them as separate entities. However, when we choose our teaching approaches as conductors we can find ourselves emphasizing one over the other (consciously or unconsciously) and in doing so we dramatically change the very nature of what we do. Unless we are aware that we ride a delicate balance every time we step on the podium we are in danger of teaching from a limited perspective and in the end shortchanging the ensemble and ourselves as well.

FOCUS ON MORE THAN TECHNIQUE

We limit ourselves if we only think of our role as trainers of skill or developers of technique. We can get caught up in teaching "the notes and rhythms," the fingerings, how to shape the vowels correctly, how to watch for precise cues—the technique list is endless. As important as all that is, we need to remember that *technique must always have a higher calling than itself.* Our job is to develop the musicians' technique as a means to something greater, something more musical and meaningful. When we attend a concert we may be awestruck by a performer's technical capability; but if that is all they have to offer we leave the performance somehow unfulfilled. How many of us have said of a very fine artist "He was really talented, but not very musical." What we have witnessed is technique for the sake of technique: ultimately, an incomplete artistic product.

This is not to deny the critical relationship of technique to the quality of the musical experience. Technique unlocks the door to higher levels of musical experience. It would be difficult if not impossible to have a musically meaningful experience as a performer or audience member if the performance is riddled with wrong notes, poor intonation and rhythmic confusion. Certainly the greater one's technical ability the more likely that the music can be heard and enjoyed. When technique is seen as a means to serving a more musical end it can be developed to a high degree within a musical, expressive context. Technique leads to high levels of artistry but it is the artistry that captivates.

When we teach from the podium we work through technical challenges within a musical context. If we stop to adjust intonation, for example, we can talk not only about physical support or the right vowel shape but also the musical energy that is needed if we are to create a truly expressive phrase. When we focus on fast sixteenth-note runs, we can and should spend time helping the ensemble develop the skill of articulating those runs but also show how these passages lead somewhere: how they form a sequence of musical ideas. Placing technique within a musical context demands higher order thinking skills and provides the musicians with a more rewarding experience than one focused on skills, drills, exercises and note pounding. Try motivating a beginning clarinetist by focusing solely on the basic technical challenges of fingering, embouchure, note-reading and scales. When we teach for technique only we are saying, in effect, "Hang in there for a few years. I know it's not interesting now but it will get better." In this era of quick results, fast food and light-speed technology, musicians are much less likely to hang in there. There are too many other things that compete for their time, talents and interest. We need to find ways to develop their technical skills by challenging their thinking as well as their fingering:

> Students will be more intellectually involved when practicing repertoire that requires higher order or divergent thinking and active problem solving than when practicing mundane drill and practice exercises. Encouraging students to come to the next lesson with five different ways of playing an exercise or to devise a set of similar exercises to overcome a technical problem will be more intrinsically motivating than merely telling them to practice an exercise until it has been mastered.[50]

As leaders we need to understand this and remember that what makes the experience compelling is not technique in itself but the *music* that is the result of good technique. Always bringing technique under the umbrella of the bigger musical picture—the phrase, the cultural/historical significance of the music, the composer's intent and the musicians' personal response to the music—will keep technique in its important but proper place.

> Even among the elite, top-tier classical musicians, there is more to being a musician than having excellent technique. Both Arthur Rubinstein and Vladimir Horowitz are widely regarded as two of the greatest pianists of the twentieth century but they made mistakes—little technical mistakes— surprisingly often. A wrong note, a rushed note, a note that isn't fingered properly. But as one critic

---

50 Parncutt and McPherson, 41.

wrote, "Rubinstein makes mistakes on some of his records, but I'll take those interpretations that are filled with passion over the twenty-two-year-old technical wizard who can play the notes but can't convey the meaning."[51]

CHOOSE REPERTOIRE THAT TEACHES AND DEVELOPS THE ENSEMBLE

Repertoire is everything. It's the textbook for the course, the curriculum for developing skill and understanding and the determiner of energy, morale and momentum in rehearsals. Everything we do and experience together as conductor and ensemble is built on the foundation of the music we study and prepare for performance.

As leaders of the experience we need to spend significant energy choosing the repertoire and designing a program that will not only produce a wonderful concert but also will inspire and challenge us in the days and weeks leading to that performance. Too often with our "product" mentality we think about the *concert* but forget that even before we get there we will spend hours, days and weeks *in rehearsal*. Ask yourself: Will the repertoire stand up to this test? Will it be interesting, offer opportunities for exploration, provide a sense of purpose and force us into uncomfortable territory and bring us back again?

That sounds pretty heady, but remember that this is relative to the age and experience level of the ensemble. A simple folksong sung in unison can be just as challenging and interesting as a multi-movement work for wind ensemble if the music suits the goals you have set for the musicians and if you lead rehearsals in a way that enables the ensemble to reach those objectives.

Choosing repertoire starts with your musical goals for the ensemble. You will have many goals and if you are to reach them

---

51   Daniel J. Levitin, *This Is Your Brain on Music* (New York: Dutton, 2006), 204.

the repertoire must provide the opportunity. Some repertoire will help musicians master certain technical skills or develop a particular kind of tone color; with other pieces the objective may be to learn to improvise within a given structure (as in jazz or aleatoric music) or to experience a style that represents a different cultural background. Sometimes the goal is just to enjoy making music, to experience a certain kind of rhythmic feel or to engage with the audience in an exciting way. You will have many goals: big and small, deeply musical and programmatically ambitious. Whatever they are let the goals guide you in choosing repertoire.

Look for music that challenges the ensemble to accomplish goals within a broader musical context. In other words, beware of pieces that are technically demanding but not very musically satisfying (a common problem in beginning ensemble repertoire). Every piece should help develop the musicians' ability to sing or play expressively, purposefully and meaningfully; that can only happen if we start with quality repertoire.

In addition to choosing music that meets your goals, choose music that you love or at least highly value. It will be very difficult for you to look forward to rehearsals if the music does not hold anything for you personally. Regardless of what you *tell* the ensemble your feelings will always come through as you rehearse the music. If you had little or no choice about the repertoire (avoid this situation at all costs), then you must at least try to find something of *value* in every piece in order to make the experience worthwhile for everyone, yourself included. Maybe you're not crazy about pop music but the board decided it wanted to do a Pops Concert for the spring fundraiser. You can just bide your time in rehearsal or you can decide to approach the music from the perspective of learning as much about what constitutes best practice for this genre. Choose the *best examples* of this music: pieces that have some musical validity and that you can relate to on some level so that rehearsals can be musically satisfying for you and for the ensemble.

The foundation for the musical experience is the *music*. As leaders of the ensemble we shape the musical experience by laying a solid foundation with quality repertoire. Whatever time and effort it takes to find great repertoire will be worth it when you step on the podium to rehearse that piece for the fifth time or to ultimately perform it as the culmination of all your work.

DESIGN REHEARSALS TO TEACH IN CONTEXT

Okay, I'll be honest. On my "top ten" list of annoyances is the conductor who goes into rehearsal without a well thought out plan. The practice, especially among many seasoned conductors, of walking (or running) into rehearsal and simply "picking up where we left off" with the score—without any specific intentions or strategies for that rehearsal—can be a recipe for boredom, inefficiency, frustration, unnecessary repetition and a sense of purposelessness. If leadership means guiding the way, then conductors who lead through their teaching must design a rehearsal to make the best use of people's time and talents.

> In short, capable conductors must be remarkably prepared and have complete knowledge of the score and how to realize it.... All aspects of the rehearsal should be planned.[52]

Planning all aspects of the rehearsal does not mean being able to predict the future but it does mean utilizing your foresight and your teaching skills to present the music and design the experience so that understanding and skill development can be maximized in the time you have. The key to making this happen is to see rehearsal as a series of wholes and parts that work in relationship along a continuum that moves us forward to a greater goal.

---

52   Parncutt and McPherson, 2002, 346.

Simply put, structuring any learning experience using a "whole-part-whole" paradigm means sharing and exploring content in context so that it can be understood, mastered and meaningful.

Whether you are beginning a rehearsal, polishing a piece, introducing a new work or leading a sectional, provide some kind of context or grounding upon which the learning will take place: something to frame the learning and provide focus and purpose. This can be a review of a section of the piece, listening to a recording, saying a few words about the historical or cultural context of the music or laying out an overriding musical goal to be accomplished that day. This first "whole" helps us see the bigger picture and provides motivation for the work ahead.

Once we have established some context for the rehearsal we can work on the details, whether this means technical agility, harmonic understanding, blending and balancing, expressiveness or simply correct notes and rhythms. But it is just as important here in the middle of the "whole-part-whole" paradigm to continue to work in context; to work out the details and develop skill and understanding against the backdrop of something larger. This means, for example, helping singers negotiate a tricky interval and then immediately placing that interval in the context of the larger line, the transitions into and out of this line and the piece as a whole. How many times have we pounded notes for one voice part without connecting this passage to what other voices are doing or to the accompaniment or to the transition that precedes it, only to become frustrated when the ensemble doesn't remember it moments or days later? Without a link or anchor, something to relate the new skill or information to, the ensemble's success in retaining what was learned is unpredictable and dependent largely on muscle memory. Asking singers to pick a note out of thin air leaves the performance to chance; teaching them to *know* where that note is based on its relationship to something else in the music means they have learned not only how to understand and be successful in *this* piece but how to apply that understanding to future musical challenges. The same can be said for instrumentalists who are drilled on a passage from a purely technical standpoint. Whether they master the passage and play it expressively will be largely determined by the context within which the learning of the technical skills took place.

Simply put, as conductors we can choose to make rehearsals drill sessions where technical and even expressive elements are rehearsed as tasks on a to-do list or we can take the time to plan our rehearsals and methods so that a broader understanding and a more musical performance takes place. When we teach and not just rehearse, and do so in context of something bigger, the music and the musicians reap the short and long-term benefits.

Once you have finished working on the passage or piece for that rehearsal it is important to put the learning into a final context. This allows everyone to assess the growth that took place and to think ahead to what else needs to be accomplished. This assessment is important not only for the conductor but also for the ensemble in order for them to take part in analyzing and evaluating its progress. Hearing, feeling and experiencing the music that final time—the final "whole"—is a satisfying experience because it is a kind of reward for the work that was done and reinforces what was learned by placing it in real time without interruptions. The final whole brings us one step closer to the performance and gives a stronger starting place for the next rehearsal on that piece. It also allows musicians to understand their role in the wider context of everyone else in the ensemble and to the finished piece.

> I think musical understanding is present when performing musicians are able to create something in which they comprehend the whole to which they are contributing their parts. So, in terms of a performing ensemble, it means the musicians understand how their parts fit into the entire composition—what

makes up the whole, what the form of the piece is, how the components of the structure relate to the way their parts are to be played… Musical understanding recognizes that context.[53]

Context provides motivation and purpose; it anchors learning and ensures understanding. As conductors we can use what I call a zoom in/zoom out approach to rehearsal: in the same way we take our camera and zoom in on an object to see its detail and then zoom out to see and experience the broader picture we can rehearse the details and shape the nuance in our music always against a backdrop of the bigger musical landscape.

CHOOSE A COLLABORATIVE APPROACH TO REHEARSAL

In Chapter One we looked at Greenleaf's best test of servant leadership as he asks "Do those served grow as persons? Do they, *while being served*, become healthier, wiser, freer, more autonomous, more likely themselves to become servants?"[54]

Let's focus for a moment on the phrase "more autonomous." Conductors value their *own* autonomy, but what about the autonomy of those we most directly serve: the musicians in our ensembles? How do we reconcile our desire to create a unified sound and oneness of mind and action with the autonomy of those we lead?

Conductor-leaders strive to develop musicians who understand how to make musical decisions and are capable of utilizing this ability in ways that contribute to the rehearsal process as well as the finished product. Understood this way, autonomy can serve both the individual's and the ensemble's goals. At the intersection of our teaching, conducting and leadership skills is our ability to develop

---

53   Larry Rachleff in Catherine Larsen's "An Interview with Larry Rachleff: The Heart and the Brain in Performing" in *Performing with Understanding* (MENC, 2000), 139–40.

54   Greenleaf, 13–14.

the musicians' independence *while at the same time* persuading them to utilize their ever-refining abilities in surrender of something greater, something they can only accomplish in collaboration with others. This is the ultimate challenge of the conductor and when accomplished, the ultimate success.

For this to happen *we must be willing to develop a collaborative teaching style and collaborative working relationship with the ensemble.* Collaboration can be a scary concept for conductors who fear letting go of any control or who seriously doubt the musicians' ability to make good artistic decisions. Maybe you conduct young children or a beginning ensemble of some kind; or perhaps you work with experienced musicians and have tried to involve them in a more participative process but with little success. Collaboration seems like a remote possibility, or more accurately a recipe for failure.

But think for a moment of what "collaboration" really means: to "co-labor," to work alongside someone (or several someones) for a mutually satisfying end result. Isn't that what we do, or would like to do: work *with* our ensemble on something we all love to create? Framed this way, the rehearsal process takes on an entirely different light. Rather than walking into rehearsal thinking we need to do something *to* the musicians, we can think about what we can do *with* the musicians: the strategies, ideas, concepts, techniques, skills and possibilities we can explore *together*. And the experiences we can enjoy *together*.

> Creativity cannot be conceptualized as being the sole prerogative of the teacher-director, the students being artisans who only carry out his or her artistic wishes. The students must share in the creativity, under the insightful, unifying governance of the teacher.[55]

---

55   Reimer, 193.

Collaboration in the rehearsal is based on three things: *sharing our insight, engaging the ensemble in meaningful ways* and *empowering musicians to contribute to the decision-making process.* Together these three actions help us to share ownership for the creative work of the ensemble *with* the ensemble.

Sharing our insight means taking the time where possible to *briefly share the reasons behind the creative decisions we make as a conductor.* So often we barrel through rehearsals firing off one directive after another, clear in our own mind about why these things make sense but rarely taking the time to let the ensemble in on our conductor's secrets. We act like members of some club with a secret handshake that can't—or won't—divulge the reasoning behind our actions. A silly analogy, perhaps, but isn't this what we often do?

For example, rather than just repeatedly correcting the ensemble to sing a unified "oo" vowel, why not take the time to *explain* how vowel unification relates to intonation? Or instead of drilling a phrase so that it obediently reflects the dynamics on the page, why not talk about melodic shape or weight, text emphasis, composer intent or whatever else might be a more musical, insightful motive for using those dynamics? We don't have to give a lengthy lecture on any subject; we can simply *help musicians begin to understand to the degree that is appropriate for their experience and ability level the kinds of decisions we face as musicians and how we go about making those decisions—to let them in on what drives the decision making process when artists create art.* Not only does this help the ensemble feel more connected to what is happening in the rehearsal but they also feel more connected to us because they begin to realize that we're not just arbitrarily asking them to do strange things; they feel important, valued and trusted because we have shared this insight with them. Sharing insight is a way of modeling for the ensemble the behaviors and understandings we want them to develop; it paves the way for growing the musicians' own abilities to make musical decisions.

A second step and natural follow-up to sharing our insight and ideas is to engage the ensemble in multiple ways. Musicians of all levels quickly become accustomed to one-way communication, to sitting and waiting to be told what to do even if they don't appreciate this passive approach. When we begin to engage them in more interesting and meaningful ways they begin to wake up (sometimes, literally) and participate in ways that make them more invested in the ensemble.

The easiest way to engage the ensemble is to ask questions instead of providing all the information and answers. If you do not routinely ask questions as part of your rehearsal, try it. Initially you may get blank stares, nervous fidgeting or frivolous responses— but you will get attention. It is unfortunate that ensembles are so unaccustomed to being legitimately asked for input (as opposed to being questioned for punitive purposes) that they don't know how to respond to your questions. In time, however, their willingness to answer questions will grow as their trust grows. When we pose questions in an almost conversational way (again, think co-labor) we help the ensemble clarify information ("What does that marking mean?"), remember a concept or skill worked on in a previous rehearsal ("What were we going to do with that phrase?") or seek out new information ("What do you think will be a challenge in this new section?"). Questions engage musicians and hold them accountable for their part in the creative process and they can lead to a discussion of new ideas or strategies.

Besides asking questions we can engage the ensemble by asking them to conduct with us, as when we are working through a tricky passage or rhythm or trying to sing or play a particularly expressive phrase. Musicians love to conduct (albeit sometimes for all the wrong, power-oriented reasons) and always respond more acutely to our gesture when they have challenged themselves as conductors. Even young or inexperienced ensembles can conduct basic gestures and when they experience first hand how tricky or fun or interesting it is they become more connected to us and to the music. When we invite more experienced or professional ensembles to conduct we validate their expertise in a way that also draws us together into a closer professional relationship.

There are many other ways to engage the ensemble in rehearsal if we just use our creativity and exploratory abilities to experiment with different ideas. Challenging them with exercises that make MENSA level demands on their ears and their minds, incorporating theoretical knowledge into the rehearsal in a way that demands they apply the knowledge or virtually anything else that takes them out of their passive zone will help create an environment of involvement and collaboration.

The final aspect of developing a collaborative approach to the rehearsal is to involve musicians in solving artistic problems. Instead of always diagnosing the problem and prescribing the solution we can invite the ensemble to take part in this process. This requires that they do two things: they must call upon their prior experience and then apply the skills and knowledge they have gained to new situations. This is at the heart of successful teaching and with our guidance can make the collaborative relationship rewarding for everyone.

Empowering the ensemble to make artistic decisions means acknowledging their ability to not only make good decisions given a musical problem but also their ability to analyze the music and find those problems in the first place—to determine what challenges exist without our help. Analyzing the music may take many different forms, depending on the age and experience of the ensemble. A collegiate percussion ensemble will be able to talk theoretically using appropriate musical terminology while a beginning orchestra may have more intuitive ways of discussing the music. In both cases the process is fundamentally the same: *the ensemble takes the music apart in some detail by looking at it, listening to it and playing or singing it in order to better understand, perform and experience it.*

By experiencing the music, evaluating their performance, analyzing the music and calling on prior experience the musicians can determine musical challenges and pose solutions. As conductors we ask more open-ended questions that demand that the detail comes from the ensemble. Instead of saying "Where should we breathe in this phrase?" we ask "How did we do on that phrase?" Because we are not posing a leading question (one that calls for a specific response) there is more autonomy given to and more responsibility placed on the musicians themselves to analyze and evaluate the process and the product during rehearsal. The ensemble feels more invested and valued because *they are more fully utilizing all their musical skills, not just the technical ones that we direct them to use in a more restricted leadership style.*

In this kind of rehearsal we become *facilitators and organizers*, guiding a group of artists in our collaborative work. We also allow musicians to take more responsibility for setting goals and charting progress. One of the best things we can do is to take time at the end of each piece or each rehearsal and talk as a group about our progress. "How did we do? What should we focus on next time? What can you do between now and then so we can meet our goal?" Questions like these open the door to real investment and ownership on the part of the ensemble. Even when rehearsal doesn't go as well as planned there is still a sense of forward momentum and direction because there are clear goals that have come from within the ensemble, not put upon them from "on high." (That would be us.) Ultimately this approach fosters a different understanding of influence and power and develops a different relationship between conductor and ensemble.

> Among its more glaring flaws, the somewhat prescriptive, teacher-directed approach in musical training emphasizes a hierarchical rather than egalitarian interrelationship between teacher and student, especially in cases of rule-covered action. Limited student input into the design of the methods employed and the ends to which they tend, and the

one-way communication from teacher to student rather than two-way between teacher and student, may breed student passivity, convergent thinking, and dependence on the expectations of significant others rather than student activity, divergent thinking, and independent action. In this event, teaching reduces to a manipulative exercise of personal power over students for musical ends rather than the judicious use of influence or power with students implied in more egalitarian relationships.[56]

In a collaborative style we share and receive insight and allow the musicians some responsibility for musical decision-making. Practically speaking, however, even with the most capable and experienced ensembles we have a limit to the amount of dialogue we can engage in during rehearsal; if we were to put up every musical decision for democratic vote we would lose all momentum and never get a piece learned. What matters is that we begin to look at the way we shape the learning of repertoire and the development of musical skill, understanding and artistry so that it leads to more engaged, invested, creative, thinking and autonomous musicians.

BE DIRECTIVE WHEN NECESSARY

By now you have begun to wonder whether you can ever just give some good, old-fashioned clear directions to your ensemble without thinking you have somehow stilted their growth or experience.

Not to worry. Whether you have been utilizing a collaborative approach for some time or you have just decided that this is something you would like to try in your conducting and teaching,

---

56 Estelle R. Jorgensen, *In Search of Music Education* (Urbana and Chicago, IL: University of Illinois Press, 1997), 12.

you no doubt realize that there are times when great leadership means we must be more directive in our approach with the ensemble. A directive (or directing) style is one conductors are most comfortable with because it is the style in which we were trained in our undergraduate programs and the style we most likely have experienced for most of our lives as members of ensembles. Put simply, a directive style is one in which the leader—the conductor in this case—diagnoses the problems and prescribes the solutions; it is a leader-centered, autocratic (but not necessarily dictatorial) approach which can be very effective and efficient. But how do we reconcile using a directive approach with a more collaborative style of leadership?

In their discussion of situational leadership, Ken Blanchard, Patricia Zigarmi, and Drea Zigarmi[57] outline four approaches to leadership which can be applied to meet the needs of those we lead or the needs of the situation. On one end of the spectrum is what they call the directing style in which "the leader provides specific direction and closely monitors task accomplishment." It is a good style to use with enthusiastic beginners—people with few skills or little experience but the potential to do well. In this style, you "tell the person [ensemble] what the goal is and what a good job looks like, but you also lay out a step-by-step plan about how the task is to be accomplished. You solve the problem. You make the decisions; the person [ensemble] carries out your ideas."[58]

For beginners, a directing style can be effective because you act as a model for the musicians: you sing or play a line and they repeat it after you. You introduce them to the experience of music making by sharing ideas, providing examples and helping them build skills in a kind of apprenticeship relationship that you steer.

A directing style may also be used with people who have a greater level of ability or experience if "a decision has to be made

---

57   Ken Blanchard, Patricia Zigarmi and Drea Zigarmi, *Leadership and the One Minute Manager* (New York: William Morrow and Company, Inc., 1985).

58   Blanchard *et al*, 30-31.

quickly and the stakes are high."[59] When we have a lot of repertoire to polish and a concert drawing near, a directing style, even with professional or highly capable amateur ensembles, may be the wise choice.

While I believe collaboration should be our primary *modus operandi*, there are times when the ensemble *needs* us to be directive in our approach or the result will be a frustrating or ineffective rehearsal. We must be aware of and respond to this paradox: that most of the musicians we work with will have a dual need for security (structure, certainty, clarity, direction) and adventure (exploration, experimentation, ownership, independence). Our ability to *assess the situation* and apply the approach that is needed at that moment— directive, collaborative or (as we shall see) delegating—is a large measure of our leadership effectiveness (hence the term "situational leadership").[60] In reality, some kind of collaboration can be used in every rehearsal, even the earliest rehearsal with beginners when we ask them to decide which of two examples sounds better and why. And every rehearsal can benefit from the momentum created by an insightful and efficient conductor *directing* our actions so that the music comes alive. Ultimately we must become comfortable blending various leadership styles so they can be used seamlessly in rehearsal as we assess and respond to the situation.

When we use a directing style we must be careful not to appear dictatorial or punitive. We can be clear, to the point and detailed without being sarcastic or cutting. Think of the directing style as our opportunity to provide the missing piece of the puzzle in a quick and effective way. Be clear in your directions and try to make your next statement an invitation to collaborate, even in some small way toward the joint effort so musicians will feel fully invested in the ensemble.

---

59   Blanchard *et al*, 1985, 36.
60   Blanchard *et al* outline four styles: directing, coaching, supporting and delegating. I have chosen to discuss coaching and supporting together as aspects of what I call a collaborative approach to leadership.

DELEGATE THOUGHTFULLY

As conductors we direct and we collaborate with musicians as we shape the music and musical experience. Sometimes we choose to develop and encourage the musicians' autonomy to the point where we "[turn] over responsibility for decision-making and problem-solving" to them—we delegate.

A delegating style may be best suited to chamber ensemble settings because it is for *"people who have both competence and commitment.* They are able and willing to work on a project by themselves with little supervision or support."[61] A delegating style may also be appropriate for larger ensembles when used for certain projects or pieces or for non-musical or administrative tasks.

Delegating seems like a non-leadership style if we think of it as giving away responsibility and virtually all control. But delegating does not mean *abdicating*. When we delegate we charge someone with acting *on our behalf*, which means *we are still a part of the enterprise*. Delegating in all settings needs some structure to be successful. *We must set clear expectations, be sure roles are defined and ensure those we delegate responsibility to determine an operating and evaluation procedure. We must also remain a part of the process, even if only as facilitator or advisor.*

I have seen chamber music groups, especially those in academic settings, completely fail because the conductor did not exercise his leadership by delegating appropriately. Simply assembling an ensemble, designating a leader and telling them to "work it out" may seem like the ingredients for a chamber music experience, but in reality we must continue to be involved, albeit in a different way, in order for the musicians to benefit from the experience. Yes, they need to explore collaborative music making with peers—a different relational endeavor than making music with a conductor. But as we saw in the prologue of this book, the need for musical independence or autonomy *co-exists* with the need for some

---

61   Blanchard *et al*, 57.

kind of direction or leadership. In a chamber music setting both needs are still operating and it is the conductor's job to facilitate this seemingly paradoxical relationship. Being completely hands-off may be appropriate if the ensemble is really interested in an exercise in interpersonal communication or conflict resolution. In reality, hands-off in chamber settings only allows us to assign blame when things don't work out. If we don't structure and facilitate according to the needs of the musicians we lead we program them for failure, or at best a mediocre experience. We need to take the time to assess the capabilities of the members of the ensemble—their experience, their ability and their temperaments—and structure the experience accordingly. For advanced or professional ensembles this may be as simple as being sure roles and goals are defined and conveying this information to everyone involved. For less experienced groups we will need to spend time teaching them how to work together and will want to check in with them regularly, helping to assess their musical and interpersonal progress to be sure things are moving forward. In every case we want to be available to act as an encourager and guide.

When we use a delegating style with chamber ensembles, musicians are responsible for taking apart the musical puzzle before them and must come to some agreement about challenges and choices—with little direct involvement by the conductor. The musicians may decide in advance to delegate particular roles within the group: one person to have ultimate authority in the area of repertoire choice, one on stylistic interpretation (based on research they have done), another on language coaching and so forth. This allows for leadership opportunities among the members of the ensemble and determines in advance how conflict will be handled when it does (and it will) occur. The better the structure and advance planning the more likely the experience will be successful and with minimal direct involvement on the conductor's part.

We can also use a delegating style with a large ensemble. Often this takes the form of delegating conducting/teaching responsibility to an assistant conductor or a student leader or officer. The same needs apply here as in a chamber music setting: we must be sure to provide structure, feedback and guidance or the individuals to whom we delegate responsibility may be unsuccessful, or worse yet may create interpersonal or musical problems where none existed before. This can happen when, for example, a high school drum major tackles her job without a thorough understanding of how to exercise authority appropriately in relation to her peers and becomes a dictator, thinking this is what it means to be in charge or responsible. Ultimately, however, *we* are responsible as conductors and leaders of the organization; when we delegate responsibility and authority we need to extend our teaching to the *teaching of leadership*. We need to work with our assistant conductors or student officers and help them understand our philosophy of leadership, the parameters of the job we have given them and how to work with fellow musicians. Only then will delegation be successful.

THE TEACHING REHEARSAL:
AN INVESTMENT FOR THE LONG RUN

Conducting brings teaching and leading together by sharing our knowledge in a way that guides a group of individuals to accomplish a goal that demonstrates, in public and in real time, the collective knowledge gained.

We do this by paying as much attention to process as to product and by balancing our time between directive and collaborative approaches, at times even delegating responsibility in answer to the needs of those we lead. We pave the way for long-term understanding as well as short-term results by teaching skills and knowledge in a wider context, by making connections to concepts and experiences that help musicians learn and then transferring that learning in meaningful ways. This kind of teaching demonstrates a choice we have made whether we realize it or not to teach for transfer of ideas, to teach for more than the next performance.

> [C]onceptual rehearsing reinforces or introduces concepts in ways that encourage the transfer of concepts from one passage to another passage or work. Statements can be as simple as "whenever you see a terraced dynamic, take care not to anticipate it with a slight crescendo or decrescendo" or as sophisticated as "this section is the recapitulation; what does that mean?" In secondary school choral settings, approximately 1% of rehearsal time is spent attempting to evoke higher order thinking, such as analysis, synthesis, or evaluation (e.g., Watkins, 1996). This same automaton like approach to rehearsing has also been found in secondary school instrumental rehearsals, where less than 3% of rehearsal time is spent in attempts to improve the grasp of musical concepts (Blocher, Greenwood, & Shellahamer, 1997). The literature, the bulk of which comes from the United States, is quite clear with regard to learning: unless one teaches for the transfer of ideas, there is no transfer.[62]

When we teach from the podium we engage musicians in the learning in such a way that they take more ownership of the process, are more challenged to provide input beyond their playing or singing and are more invested in the experience. Instead of using one-way communication that allows musicians to respond to us like automatons, we demand more of them by calling upon their higher order thinking skills. Historically, however, this is not the case:

---

62   Parncutt and McPherson, 342.

While considerable proportions of rehearsals are spent in verbal activity and modeling, principally on the part of the conductor, little of it elicits higher order or conceptual thinking on the part of the performers. General music and ensemble classes generally involve students in lower cognitive processes, emphasizing mechanics of performance almost to the exclusion of the application and accumulation of musical knowledge and the abilities to think about music (Goodlad, 1983). Conductors' efforts appear to be weighted toward providing guidance on how to make corrections or presenting exact solutions, by saying things such as "you need more air" or "the percussion need to play softer." This limits opportunities for self-correction on the part of the ensemble through slight hints or scaffolding (Weeks, 1996). In these situations, ensemble members function much like simple machinery, rendering only specific responses to specific instructions about a specific point in a specific piece of music.[63]

If we are one-dimensional in our approach to teaching from the podium we are missing opportunities for the ensemble to grow. Though a directive style can be efficient it is not necessarily the style that creates the deepest or most meaningful experience for those we lead because it can limit their input and creativity. As musicians develop they want and need different things from the ensemble experience and if they don't get them their development and their work ethic can suffer. Like a parent who controls a child's every move and then becomes frustrated when he won't take responsibility, the conductor who limits her work to a directing

---

63   Parncutt and McPherson, 342.

style will eventually become frustrated when the ensemble doesn't seem invested enough in the artistic process. *Why won't they come to rehearsal regularly? Why don't they look at their music outside of rehearsal and show at least some initiative or interest in the welfare of the ensemble? Why don't they care as much as I care?*

The answer, I believe, is at least partially due to the fact that when we use a directing style exclusively the musicians tend to see the organization as the conductor's ensemble, not theirs. Why should musicians bother to think, to take musical risks or to be expressive (all things we ask of them) if the conductor is going to make all the decisions and judgments anyway? Why should they invest any more time, energy or self in this process when all that matters is their ability to execute certain tasks on command?

It is precisely this frustration and dissatisfaction that has led many organizations, including musical organizations like Orpheus Chamber Ensemble, to explore and employ more engaging, empowering and collaborative approaches to organizational work. Instead of being limited by a directing style leaders in these organizations have turned the tables on traditional, autocratic approaches and opened up the process of creation in ways that involve the members of the organizations in simple or sometimes highly responsible ways.

A collaborative style may take more time than a directing style where the diagnostic-prescriptive approach is exclusively used. But this time is an investment in not only the short-term product (a performance characterized by better understanding of the music) but also the long-term development of the musicians and the ensemble as a whole. Empowering musicians to make some creative decisions means being open to a new vision for the piece than the one we ourselves created, but this collective vision can lead not only to a better performance but one charged with the energy of the X Factor we talked about in Chapter Three.

The rehearsal atmosphere must be such that the combination of conductor persuasiveness and collaboration results in an ensemble that is responsive and receptive to the conductor's verbal and nonverbal behaviors. Indeed, performances appear to benefit when ensemble members feel a part of the learning process rather than functioning as passive recipients of information (Hamann et al., 1990).[64]

Even though it appears that there is little encouragement of higher order thinking and the development of concepts in rehearsals, it would seem that planning and employing strategies to promote these throughout the rehearsal would be most effective in the long-term growth of performers and ensembles. Without these attributes, a conductor is condemned to re-teach an idea every time a similar passage or concept is encountered, as opposed to musicians making connections cognitively and transferring knowledge and skills to new situations. More sophisticated performers have likely attained higher order music skills through inductive reasoning as a result of synthesis of many experiences; thus conductors of highly skilled ensembles are better able to attend to the performance nuances that help make music rapturous.[65]

Rather than complain that we don't have very good musicians in our ensembles or envy those conductors who do, we can plan

---

64 Parncutt and McPherson, 336.
65 Parncutt and McPherson, 343.

and employ strategies to develop sophisticated performers which can lead us to performances of rapturous music. We don't have to wait until they have amassed experience in someone else's ensembles before they can be effective in ours or see ourselves as preparers of musicians who will someday make connections, but not while they are with us. Yes, we are all a link in the chain, each playing a role in the life cycle of a musician. But wherever we are, whatever musicians we have, whatever their ability and experience, we can set a standard for ourselves and for them by using more conceptual, experiential, contextual teaching in rehearsal and expecting that the result will be more thoughtful, insightful and meaningful music making.

THE TEACHING CONDUCTOR AS SERVANT-LEADER

Have you ever felt like you were in someone else's dream, watching the dreamer have a great time, all the while wondering "But what about me? What about *my* experience?"

When as conductors we go about business as usual, directing all the moves of the musicians in our ensemble, we become the dreamer—and our ensemble asks "But what about us? What about *our* experience?" They may not voice that sentiment; they may not even be consciously aware of the source of their discontent, but through their actions and their attitudes they daily ponder the question. In time they forget there was even a question to be asked and they just go about the same routine in a kind of fog.

Musicians can get so accustomed to being told what to do that they become aesthetically and intellectually numb. If engaged in only the most perfunctory way in the rehearsal they function on autopilot and, even while looking like they are involved can be a million miles away. If we are going to teach them, *engage them*, help them grow in multiple ways and provide the opportunity for meaningful musical experience, we need to give up some of the control and find creative ways to balance efficiency with experience;

to maintain our leadership role while trusting that the ensemble has a greater place in the process than to just sound notes.

In his classic book *The Courage to Teach*, Parker Palmer shows how underestimating our students (in a sense, anyone we lead) means choosing teaching strategies or approaches that reflect our lack of faith in their ability, potential and curiosity:

> [O]ur assumption that students are brain-dead leads to pedagogies that deaden their brains. When we teach by dripping information into their passive forms, students who arrive in the classroom alive and well become passive consumers of knowledge and are dead on departure when they graduate. But the power of this self-fulfilling prophecy seems to elude us: we rarely consider that our students may die in the classroom because we use methods that assume they are dead.[66]

"Dripping information into their passive forms" is what we do when we bore musicians to death by our unilateral approach to rehearsal; when we direct every move, make every decision, determine every outcome and make no attempts to creatively design rehearsals or learning experiences to involve the ensemble in a deeper way. The musicians not only lose the ability to be involved on multiple levels; they lose hope that this may ever be possible. Unless we make a major shift in our thinking about the way we teach as conductors we will never come close to experiencing the potential of the music, the musicians and the process we share.

There are no perfect teachers, no perfect conductors and no one-size-fits-all prescriptions for leading rehearsals. There is only the challenge to fine tune our awareness, to dedicate ourselves and step out of our routine in order to determine what the ensemble

---

66   Parker J. Palmer, 42.

needs to move ahead in its growth. Whether or not you want your ensemble to function like a chamber ensemble or to perform without a conductor, you should want them to *have the ability to do so.* This is the autonomy that Greenleaf speaks about, the growth that occurs when we have really done our jobs as leaders and, I would add, as teachers from the podium. By expanding our approach to teaching we can move towards more creative involvement, more growth and more independence. It is not easy; it takes time, dedication and consistent evaluation of and reflection on our work. But it seems to me it is the only choice if we are to maximize our influence as leaders and teachers throughout our conducting lives.

Teaching is the foundation for our leadership as conductors. It affords us the opportunity to share our knowledge of and passion for music with people who will play a significant role in the experience. Teaching is service in action because through teaching we are guiding and growing the musicians and hopefully helping them to be "wiser, freer, [and] more autonomous"[67] in their pursuit of musical excellence.

---

67   Greenleaf, 13.

ZOOM IN / ZOOM OUT ～

The variety of ways in which we can interact with our ensembles—the styles of leading, the approaches we take to unveiling the music, how we spend our time in rehearsal—require that we have what I call "zoom in/zoom out awareness." We limit our teaching effectiveness, the ensemble's progress and ultimately our joint artistry by staying focused on only one mode of operating. Many of us have gotten so good at "getting our act down" that we are blind to the possibilities we could see by zooming in on detail and technique at a deeper level or by zooming out to bigger picture thinking and broader musical understanding. Facing the musical landscape of extraordinary possibility, we can focus on the wider coastline or on the detail of a shell in the foreground. In reality both are beautiful, both are necessary to the complete experience. It is our discernment and planning that leads us to choosing where our focus is at any point in time and therefore where we will direct the focus of our ensemble.

> And I think the greatness of a performing musician is directly tied to his preoccupation with detail. The difficulty is to treat each detail as if it were the most important element and yet, not lose sight of the whole piece. It's very easy to do one or the other, but really combining the two is not easy.[68]

---

68 Daniel Barenboim and Edward W. Said, *Parallels and Paradoxes: Explorations in Music*

Use zoom in/zoom out thinking as a check for yourself. When you find yourself so focused on details that you have lost sight of the bigger picture take a breather and view the piece in a new way, an exercise that will inevitably lead to a fresh perspective for you and the ensemble, especially necessary when you feel you have hit a plateau. And on the flip side, if you find the music lacks clarity or the level of excellence that you want to achieve it may mean you need to zoom in on the details—the techniques, the phrasing, the moments you can freeze and shape for exquisite sound—in order for it to fully come to a place of beauty.

As the leader of the ensemble you are the artist who shapes not only the sound but the experience, so use your artist's eyes and direct attention and effort where it is most needed. If you take the time you will know which way to zoom for the best possible perspective.

---

and Society (New York: Pantheon Books, 2002), 54.

CHAPTER FIVE

LEAD BY PERSUASION ∼

*Persuasion is the process of changing or reinforcing
attitudes, beliefs, or behavior.*

—Harry Mills

Getting what we want: a universal but sometimes ugly drive of human nature. (Oops. Did I actually write that?)

We may as well start this chapter on an honest note. Let's face it: we want a lot as conductors and as leaders. We want our ensembles to make excellent music and we want them to do it our way. We have a vision for our organization: we know how the music should sound, how rehearsals will run, what performances must look like, even how administrative business should be handled. We have strong personalities, a lot of energy and passion to drive our actions. *Get out of our way.*

But there is a problem. Everything that we have already covered in this book challenges us to be a different kind of leader, to rethink the autocratic, conductor-centered, one-dimensional approach to leadership typically found in conductor/ensemble settings. We have been exploring ways to create an alternative kind of leadership based on collaboration and trust; but our experience tells us that people don't always want what we want the way we want it. Our personalities, our vision, our ways of looking at the world collide with theirs, and even when they are supposed to follow our lead they sometimes don't. What then?

We have to learn how to use our power of persuasion.

In his book *Artful Persuasion*, Harry Mills defines persuasion as "the process of changing or reinforcing attitudes, beliefs, or behavior."[69] Stop and think for a moment about how often we are in a position to persuade people—to influence their attitudes, beliefs or behavior—as conductors. At the heart of our job is our ability to move a group of musicians to think as one so that they can perform as one. But because persuasion exists on a continuum from encouragement and reinforcement on one end toward passionate debate or rationalization in the middle to blatant coercion on the opposite end, it is too simplistic to think of persuasion as a single trait or skill that we employ. How we use our powers of persuasion, whether subtle or overt, others-oriented or inherently selfish, is a reflection of our understanding of our role as influencers and our perspective on the use of our power and authority as leaders.

This chapter is about these critical challenges in our conductor lives—power, authority, coercion and persuasion—and how they can dramatically impact the way we lead.

COERCION AS MODUS OPERANDI

Continuing with our honesty approach, let us analyze what typically happens when we want something—or more specifically when we want something from the ensemble and they are not giving it to us. This can be as simple as the fifth grade choir not paying attention in rehearsal or the high school marching band not memorizing its sets despite the looming competition.

Our initial reaction is one of frustration and self-interest. Our emotions say "You're not doing what I told you to do; you're resisting me and challenging me. Well, I'm going to come out on

---

69   Harry Mills, *Artful Persuasion: How to command attention, change minds, and influence people* (New York: Amacom, 2000), 2.

top in this situation, and therefore *I will display my power and use my authority by coercing you to do what I want.*"

That's it. That is the unconscious tape that plays at lightning speed in our minds and catapults us into action. It sounds harsh (perhaps you're thinking "I don't *coerce* middle school children"), but in reality *any time we use force or punishment or deprivation or cutting sarcasm to get a result we are coercing.*

While coercion usually means forcing people to do something against their will, it can also mean using authoritative, negative or pressuring tactics, however subtle, to achieve a goal they *do* want. By refusing to do things our way they threaten our goals, so we threaten them. And back and forth it goes: both sides operating from a position of fear, defensiveness and the need to *win.* Unfortunately, even if we do win it can come at a great cost.

> At one level, followers follow out of fear—they are afraid of what might happen to them if they don't do what they are asked to do. This may be called *coercive power.* The leader in this case has created a fear in the follower that either something bad is going to happen to them or something good will be taken away from them if they do not comply. So out of fear of potentially adverse consequences, they acquiesce and "get along by going along" or by giving "lip service loyalty," at least initially. But their commitment is superficial and their energies can quickly turn to sabotage and destruction when "no one is looking" or when the threat is no longer present.[70]

Extra rehearsals, privileges taken away; negative, sarcastic comments or humor; attacks on self-esteem, cancelled performances;

---

70 Covey, 101–102.

arbitrary use of grading, threats to remove solos or chair positions; threats to call mom and dad—we do whatever it takes until we get our desired result.

Coercion is so much a part of our conductor heritage that we rarely stop to question it. When we were growing up—perhaps even now, if you still play or sing in an ensemble—it was a given that we would be punished with extra rehearsals if we didn't shape up. And the folklore surrounding conductor personalities supports coercive tactics. Great artists are always excused for their temper tantrums and forceful natures. In business circles there are still those who think that being a strong leader necessitates being a jerk. In a recent *Time* magazine article called "No Jerks Allowed" author Lisa Takeuchi Cullen bemoans the trend toward getting rid of jerks from the workplace:

> Sure, beastly bosses have shaved months off my life. But they have also been some of the most gifted people I've known. This correlation occurs with reason: talented people can get away with much worse behavior.[71]

Somehow we have not only accepted coercive behavior but even encouraged it in an odd sort of way by modeling it with our own ensembles and by warning our musicians about real life: when they go off to college or into the professional world where Maestro Ego will really let them have it if they don't toe the line (we say with almost an enviable glint in our eye). What is that all about?

It's about a dated, cowardly and ultimately ineffective way of dealing with people; dated because leaders are thinking differently about their approach to leadership today; cowardly because it avoids the real problem, which might in fact be our own inabilities, our lack of vision and planning or our inappropriate way of dealing with

---

71   Lisa Takeuchi Cullen, "No Jerks Allowed," *Time* magazine, Vol. 169, No. 14, April 2, 2007, 52.

CHAPTER FIVE: LEAD BY PERSUASION

people; ultimately ineffective because coercive tactics never bring about lasting, deep-rooted change, which means we must continue to resort to the same throw-our-weight-around approach every time the pressure is on.

> Coercive power is based on fear in both the leader and the follower. Leaders tend to lean on coercive power when they are afraid they won't get compliance. It is the "big stick" approach. It is an approach that few publicly support but may use, either because it seems justified in the face of other, bigger threats hovering over the leader or it is the expedient thing to do and seems to work at the time. But its effectiveness is an illusion.[72]

If this sounds overly dramatic or if you think this happens only in certain settings, think again. Coercive approaches are common in our profession at all age levels and in all settings. They may be subtle, they may be chalked up to the conductor's personality and they may seem justified because "this is a really tough group this year" or "it's concert week pressures," but they are always a sign of something deeper that needs to be recognized and addressed. Coercion might be a temporary fix but the real problem remains. And while we can fool ourselves into thinking we have things under control the problem is like a bug the medicine didn't quite kill: it keeps coming back, each time stronger than ever.

> The trouble with coercive power is that it only strengthens resistance. And, if successful, its controlling effect lasts only as long as the force is strong. It is not organic.[73]

---

72 Covey, 103.
73 Greenleaf, 42.

Ultimately coercive power stands in the way of getting important things accomplished and leaves everyone including the leader empty and anxious. Organizational expert Margaret Wheatley believes coercive approaches are counter to the way life is naturally designed to work:

> Western cultural views of how best to organize and lead (the majority paradigm in use in the world) are contrary to what life teaches. Western practices attempt to dominate life; we want life to comply with human needs rather than working as partners. This disregard for life's dynamics is alarmingly evident in today's organizations. Leaders use control and im position rather than self-organizing processes. They react to uncertainty and chaos by tightening already feeble controls, rather than engaging our best capacities in the dance. Leaders use primitive emotions of fear, scarcity, and self-interest to get people to do their work, rather than the more noble human traits of cooperation, caring, and generosity. This has led us to this difficult time, when nothing seems to work as we want it to, when too many of us feel frustrated, disengaged, and anxious.[74]

If we are to truly lead from the podium, then rethinking coercive tactics is a big part of our shape-up plan. We need to reflect on our perspective on power, learn why we use coercive approaches and ultimately devise alternative ways of dealing with conflict or challenges when they do arise.

---

74   Margaret J. Wheatley, *Finding Our Way: Leadership For An Uncertain Time* (San Francisco, CA: Berrett-Koehler Publishers, Inc., 2005), 1–2.

PERSPECTIVES ON POWER—
AS YOU THINK, SO SHALL YOU LEAD

Some of the most compelling essays I have read in my research on leadership have been on the use of power. Indeed, it is a topic that cannot be avoided when understanding leadership or human interaction of any kind because every relationship involves subtle and not-so-subtle displays of power in an ever-shifting dance of control, often influenced by the role authority or position plays in the power relationship.

That is why it is important to note at the outset of this discussion on persuasion that your viewpoint on power is going to be colored by your general philosophy about life, people, spirituality and the workplace as well as your own personal self-esteem. If you think of your interactions with others including the musicians you lead as presenting a kind of WIN-LOSE challenge you will approach your understanding of leadership in a very different way than if you are open to the possibility that life can present WIN-WIN scenarios. Consider the differences in these discussions of power, the first an excerpt from Robert Greene's *The 48 Laws of Power*.

> You must seduce others into *wanting* to move in your direction. A person you have seduced becomes your loyal pawn. And the way to seduce others is to operate on their individual psychologies and weaknesses. Soften up the resistant by working on their emotions, playing on what they hold dear and what they fear.[75]

The words *seduce, pawn, weaknesses* and *fear* give the reader a clear indication of the kind of perspective on power Greene presents in his lengthy work. While there are often important and insightful points

---

75   Robert Greene, *The 48 Laws of Power* (New York: Penguin Putnam Inc., 1998), 367.

made in this book, the emphasis is on manipulating and weakening others and on a kind of scarcity mentality—there's only so much good to go around and you had better grab it before someone else does. James M. Kouzes and Barry Z. Posner call this kind of thinking archaic:

> Traditional thinking promotes the archaic idea that power is a fixed sum: if I have more, then you have less. Naturally, people with this view hold tightly to the power that they perceive is theirs and are extremely reluctant to share it with anyone. This notion is wrongheaded and clearly inconsistent with all the evidence on high-performing organizations.[76]

Stephen Covey presents power in a different light:

> The more a leader is honored, respected, and genuinely regarded by others, the more legitimate power he will have with others. Depending on how leaders deal with others (which includes both real and perceived intent, interactive capacity, and interactive history), the honor followers extend to them will increase or decrease and the legitimate power in the relationship will increase or decrease. To be honorable is to have power.[77]

Covey goes on to list ten processes and principles that leaders can follow to increase their honor and therefore, their power, including:

---

76 Kouzes and Posner, 285–6.
77 Covey, 107.

112

Persuasion, which includes sharing reasons and rationale, making a strong case for your position or desire while maintaining genuine respect for followers' ideas and perspective; tell why as well as what; commit to stay in the communication process until mutually beneficial and satisfying outcomes are reached.[78]

Persuasion instead of seduction; respecting others' ideas as opposed to making them your pawn—where do you stand? Examine your own belief system as it relates to the power you wield as a conductor. Reflect on the ways in which you use your persuasive abilities with your ensemble and whether you are guilty of using coercive approaches. Ask yourself: *How do I handle my power?*

If you find you do not like the answer to that question you may need to dig further. Do you doubt your own effectiveness as a teacher, conductor or more generally, a person? Conductors are not immune to uncertainty and threats to their self-worth. Karl Albrecht describes how doubts about ourselves are reflected in our leadership of others:

Trying to function in an authority role challenges a person's emotional intelligence and social intelligence at the same time. Many leadership experts contend that people with relatively low emotional intelligence—as characterized by low self-confidence and diminished feelings of self-worth—tend to "hide behind the badge." Lacking the necessary confidence or skills to explain their views, persuade others of the soundness of their

---

78   Covey, 107.

decisions, and solve problems collaboratively, they may use their authority to intimidate others. The fearful or insecure manager may suppress dissent, reject the ideas of team members, scold and criticize them, and maintain a distant relationship with them, primarily out of a fear of loss of control.[79]

In the end we need to remember that as much as conductors are revered, respected or feared for their power the reality is that *the individual musicians are the ones who have ultimate power* over the sound that is produced. They are in control of what Daniel Barenboim calls the "initial impulse of sound."

And therefore, when one speaks about the feeling of power in the actual act of making music, the conductor has to understand what the nature of sound is: that he can change everything around it, but the actual sound, in the end, is made by the musicians. In an ideal situation, this will also keep the conductor's ego within bounds; and it will also give the individual musician in the orchestra the feeling that he is not just following orders, that he's not just an instrument for somebody else's feeling of power or determination, but that he's being very creative about it, too.[80]

Our real power as conductors lies in the power of persuasion: the ability to bring great music from a group of musicians whether it's the community chorus or the collegiate orchestra. Our

---

79   Albrecht, 212.
80   Daniel Barenboim and Edward W. Said, 71.

real challenge as conductors is to learn to use our power wisely and effectively in ways that accomplish goals by maximizing the potential of our musicians and minimizing the need for our own self-edification. Only by using power selflessly do we use it wisely; only by persuading passionately do we erase the need to coerce ruthlessly.

KEYS TO PERSUASION
GET READY FOR THE HEAT!

"On schedule." The very words generate drops of perspiration.

In Chapter Three we talked about the need to be consistent in our behavior and approach in order to gain trust from the ensemble. But while it is easy to be consistent when things are going well, it is quite another thing when the calendar is staring us in the face and we are nowhere near ready for the next performance. This is when conductors typically become "other creatures," when we snap at people, use sarcastic or cutting remarks or just blow up because we feel the walls closing in on us. We feel the heat.

The truth is, *the best time to show our true colors as conductors is in moments of adversity.* Rather than excusing ourselves for our tantrums and justifying our behavior later as normal under the circumstances we must be honest with ourselves and realize that our use of coercive tactics is most often the result of our shortcomings—our lack of preparation and vision, most often. Not taking the time to plan and prepare, to pose scenarios and work through envisioned challenges before they become reality means we find ourselves experiencing challenges when time is short and that creates stress—for us and for the ensemble. Under stress, we tend to act in ways and say things that we often regret later and that whittle away at our relationships with others. But we often feel this cycle is inevitable; we feel helpless and have convinced ourselves that "that's just the way it is" in performance settings (especially the week before the concert).

> It is relatively easy, when push comes to shove and the pressures are on, to lean on position or status or credentials or affiliations or size to force someone else to follow. And in the absence of well-developed interactive skills, or the capacity to remain true to deeply held values under pressure or a history of integrity and trust with others, it is almost impossible not to resort to force when a leader is in the middle of a crisis.[81]

What we need to remember is that *we always have choices*. Despite the circumstances we don't have to feel powerless and desperate and take our frustration out on the ensemble by reacting in a coercive, authoritarian manner. If we exercise our vision, have and use a Plan B, work on relationships with the musicians from the very beginning and continue cultivating these relationships we will know that we always have choices and that those choices will lead us to a positive resolution no matter the situation.

We will cope much better with the heat in our professional lives if we can learn to do two things: *expect the* Crisis du Jour and *accept the* Annoyances du Jour. Being ready for—indeed, *expecting*—major and minor problems has the advantage of putting us in the driver's seat, at least in terms of the way we react to problems when they arise. What causes us to be defensive and to grasp at any power tactic is our sense of losing control, of being a victim of circumstance rather than being somehow capable of effecting change. No, we do not know what might happen tomorrow, but if we understand and fully embrace the fact that each day will likely bring if nothing else some minor annoyances and at other times major challenges we don't need to feel thoroughly undone and at a loss when they do arise.

---

81   Covey, 105.

There will always be "heat" in an artistic enterprise; indeed, the absence of heat or challenge usually results in a dull product. But it is our ability to minimize the heat by our vision and planning and then respond appropriately to the heat when it does come that prevents us from using coercive tactics.

REMEMBER YOUR POWER; BE JUDICIOUS WITH YOUR AUTHORITY

The words power and authority are often used interchangeably though there is an important distinction to be made. While power can mean influence, pressure, force or persuasion, authority refers to the *right* to make a decision, as when a conductor decides which musician will play the solo.

Power is not necessarily linked to title, rank, position or decision-making ability. Everyone holds some kind of power, even if only in the way they argue their point of view in a debate or hold back information as a bargaining tool in a transaction. As conductors we have power but we also have the *authority* to make decisions; we are responsible in fact to make numerous decisions and people depend on us to take action.

Most people including conductors view authority in negative terms. Authority figures are the boss, are over us or above us in the hierarchy; they can and sometimes do threaten our success or level of contentment by their ability to change the course of things by one decision. In short, unless authority is built on principled leadership, trust relationships and shared goals it can mean autocracy at its worst.

Why is it important to make the distinction between power and authority? Because we need to realize that *we can go very far in getting the work of the ensemble accomplished using our power without necessarily resorting to our authority*. When we inspire and engage people, move them to our way of thinking by sharing our vision or painting a clear description of the goal we are using our power of persuasion without coercing or pulling rank. Stephen Covey describes this kind of power as "principle-centered power," which is:

> [T]he power some people have with others because others tend to believe in them and in what they are trying to accomplish. They are trusted. They are respected. They are honored. And they are followed because others want to follow them, want to believe in them and their cause, want to do what the leader wants. This is not blind faith, mindless obedience, or robotic servitude; this is knowledgeable, whole-hearted, uninhibited commitment. This is *principle-centered power*.[82]

When we try to stand only on our authority and not on our inherent ability to persuade we are like a three-legged chair—wobbly. Ironically, "because I am the conductor and what I say, goes" can simultaneously display authority and a *lack of true power* if we have been unable to move people effectively in other ways.

> Principle-centered power is not forced, it is invited, as the personal agendas of both leader and follower are encompassed by a larger purpose. Principle-centered power occurs when the cause or purpose or goal is believed in as deeply by the followers as by the leaders.[83]

Of course there are times and situations that warrant our use of authority, as when we are new teachers in a school that has a history of misconduct or violence. This was my situation when I was a first-year teacher. The rules in the high school where I taught

---

82 Covey, 102.
83 Covey, 104.

were strict and there was very little gray area in handling any kinds of behavioral problems. I relied on my authority to get me through tough situations, but that first year was not a smooth one by any means. It wasn't until I fully utilized my *persuasive power*—my passion, energy, vision and teaching ability—and built relationships with the students and staff that we were really successful as a choral program and happy as a community of musicians.

Remember, you hold a great deal of legitimate power as a conductor. You can move people by the sheer strength of your passion, your words and your ability to inspire and excite people through compelling music. Using your power this way, you are building and shaping something of lasting value. If you rely on authority to move people to action, it is only a band-aid that creates a tenuous feeling for you and the ensemble because there is little real foundation on which to build the organization.

USE PASSION TO PERSUADE, NOT COERCE

If we can learn to deal with the heat and to use our authority in a judicious way, then we need to learn to move people—persuade them—in a non-dictatorial way. I believe the key lies in one characteristic always ascribed to great leaders: they lived and worked with *passion*.

When Lisa Takeuchi Cullen acknowledged the talent of the jerk in the workplace, she went on to say "I don't want to enable monsters. In fact, I don't want to interact with them. But neither do I want to work in an office staffed solely with smiley faces."[84] Agreed. Who wants a plastic environment led by those who possess the skills and personality equivalent of Muzak?

What Cullen and others have not yet experienced is the leader who knows how to use her talent, conviction and energy to persuade people to action while creating an environment that encourages

---

84   Cullen, 52.

and generates productivity; the leader who uses her passion in a way that works *for* people and not *on* people.

The dictionary describes passion as "an intense emotion" or a "great liking or enthusiasm" and being passionate as "showing or inspired by strong emotion." The word "enthusiasm" is derived from the Greek for "being possessed or filled by a god."

Passion can be expressed in a multitude of ways, not all of them healthy or appropriate. Certainly the classic image of the passionate (read fiery, headstrong, baton-throwing) conductor doesn't really mesh with the leadership model we have built in this book. And while passionate doesn't necessarily mean egocentric, in our profession there is often a strong connection between the two. So the question is: How do we unleash our passion while keeping ego in check?

One of the best explanations I have read is by John P. Schuster in his essay "Servants, Egos, and Shoeshines: A World of Sacramental Possibility."[85] In describing the leader's internal character tug-of-war, he writes:

> One tricky part of servant/self-based leadership is that the ego never can be annihilated, and the juicy and energizing ego drives to compete, to win, to kick butt, to show off and strut your stuff—all these sources of passion and raw energy and creativity—can't just be shut off like water coming out of the shower spout.[86]

Schuster talks of the ego here as the fuel that makes it possible for us to be effective and creative as leaders; it is the source of strong emotion or belief in what we do and the desire to do it to the best of our ability. The ego is the awareness of the self and how the world

---

85   John P. Schuster in *Insights on Leadership: Service, Stewardship, Spirit, and Servant-Leadership*, ed. by Larry C. Spears (New York: John Wiley & Sons, Inc.), 1998, 272.

86   Schuster in Spears, *Insights on Leadership*, 272.

feels to us as *selves*. Conductors *need* egos if we are to be passionate and compelling in our creative work. The ego says "This matters to me." How much life, vitality, or inspiration would there be in our music if we turned off our egos completely? And how moved would the ensemble be if we stood on the podium completely devoid of ego? People are not likely to follow our lead if we don't feel strongly about where we are going. Put simply, if it doesn't matter to us and if people can't tell that it matters to us it won't matter to them either.

Having a healthy ego, however, is not license to step all over people and call it a necessary by-product of creative work. A healthy ego turns into a destructive force at the point when "what matters to me is more important than what matters to you; in fact, it's more important than you, yourself." When our desires, no matter how artistic or noble are held in higher esteem than the people we lead, we are in a precarious place.

> The middle path for servant leaders is to avoid the extremes of either being driven by an out-of-control ego that has power and does harm—the usual pitfall for institutional leaders—or creating a blissful self that expresses peace and harmony but is ineffectual in the world.[87]

This is a powerful statement because it helps us to better understand that the kind of leadership we have been talking about in this book is not an artificial, unrealistic, "blissful self" kind of leadership—what many people envision when they think about servant leadership or principle-centered leadership. What we have been talking about is embracing a leadership approach that shifts focus away from self and toward others—individuals and the

---

87   Schuster in Spears, *Insights on Leadership*, 273.

institutions they comprise, such as musicians and ensembles—in order to accomplish something greater than all of us. And yes, we want to accomplish something great; our passion, our ego can imagine no other way.

In *Good to Great*, Jim Collins and his team conducted extensive research on companies who had made the leap from good to great and developed a pyramid of leadership traits with the top level, Level 5, describing the kind of leader found in the great companies. The Level 5 leader is described as one who "[b]uilds enduring greatness through a paradoxical blend of personal humility and professional will."

> Level 5 leaders channel their ego needs away from themselves and into the larger goal of building a great company. It's not that Level 5 leaders have no ego or self-interest. Indeed, they are incredibly ambitious—*but their ambition is first and foremost for the institution, not themselves.*[88]

As conductors our challenge is to incorporate into our intense passion for music *a similar passion for the people with whom we create music in order that we might all together reach a high musical, artistic and expressive goal.* And when we find ourselves dreaming of the kind of ensemble we can build we need to keep ourselves in check to be sure that we are not seeing this creation as somehow a monument to ourselves and our personal ability but rather as an organization that is owned by everyone—musicians, audiences, boards—and reflective of all our efforts.

---

88   Collins, 21.

The best servant-leaders are filled with the grace
of the spirit/self, directing them to good, and are
passionate warriors with strong egos that give them
the drive to acquire and use power. This bimodal
grace/ego reality leads to the internal war servant-
leaders carry on within themselves, knowing that
power and influence will accompany them on their
journey, and that empowering others and distributing
the capacity to influence is their charter.[89]

The internal war that Schuster talks about is something we
never really conquer. But we do get better at curbing the will of
the ego (usually focused on product) when we finally realize and
accept that everything on our musical wish list involves *people* and
the relationships we forge with those people (moving our focus
more towards process). Our ego wants an excellent performance;
our spirit works to find ways to empower our ensemble to create
an excellent performance. Where once we would drill, lecture
and coerce our way to an end product, we now teach, unveil
and inspire.

Human beings are so made that whenever anything
fires the soul, impossibilities vanish. A fire in the heart
lifts everything in your life. That's why passionate
leaders are so effective. A leader with great passion
and few skills always outperforms a leader with great
skills and no passion.[90]

---

89   Schuster in Spears, *Insights on Leadership*, 273.
90   John C. Maxwell, *The 21 Indispensable Qualities of a Leader* (Nasvhille, Thomas Nelson
     Publishers, 1999), 85.

SET HIGH EXPECTATIONS
AND PERSUADE DAILY TO REACH THEM

Setting high expectations for the ensemble means persuading them from the very beginning of your relationship and then each day following that they have what it takes to get the job done at a very high level. Persuasion means changing minds, and changing people's minds about *themselves* and what they are capable of accomplishing is an integral part of every conductor's leadership.

A case in point:

In the early part of my career I was a high school choral director. I had just moved to a new position and found that one of the choirs I was to conduct was the Men's Chorus. This was truly an eclectic group: everything from freshman boys whose voices had not yet changed to juniors and seniors (two of whom later served time for grand theft auto—no kidding) that were failing out of every other class and needed an easy A. The Men's Chorus had quite the reputation for being a goof-off group, assisted, I came to find out, by the antics of the school's band and orchestra conductors. Every once in a while one of these directors would pass by the choir room during the men's rehearsal, open the doors and yell "bus crash"—a signal to the men to rumble in their chairs and to literally fall over as though they had just crashed into something. Unfortunately this was the only thing the chorus did well together.

Because these men had never been taken seriously before they were never expected to perform on their own. They had always lumbered through learning a few songs that they would sing in concert with the men of the advanced ensemble, Concert Choir. This was a way of hiding them while minimally providing an "experience." But it was clear to me that many of their behavior problems and musical inabilities were due to a lack of expectations; if you have been told you are a loser you will usually act like one. If there is no need to do well because other people will cover up for you, why bother to learn anything? It was no wonder this was such a dreaded group.

Coming into this new position, I had no intention of babysitting a group of high school boys under the guise of a men's ensemble. I made it clear in no uncertain terms the very first day that we were going to sing and learn about music—*and that we were going to do it better than anyone could imagine.*

Initially the freshmen were scared to death and the older students were skeptical, to put it mildly. I had to be pretty firm in those first several weeks, constantly reinforcing any positive behaviors I could find (and there were not many) while refusing to accept anything that would stand in the way of our success. But I also did two other things that surprised these young men. First I told them they would be performing in the fall concert *by themselves.* This was unheard of, preparing three pieces they would have to perform without the aid, or more truthfully, the camouflage of the older, experienced singers. But I knew they could do it, and I told them so—every day.

The second thing that surprised them came in the form of concert attire. In exploring the department's storage closets I found an entire set of white dinner jackets, in good shape once they would be dry-cleaned. I told the men they would need a white shirt and black pants ("black socks and shoes, too, gentlemen"), but that I would provide the rest. Somehow they complied.

The night of the concert was one I will never forget, though it was more than twenty-five years ago as I write this. Each one of these men arrived, donned the white dinner jacket and fresh lapel carnation waiting for them, walked out on stage (scared, it's true) and performed for the first time in years as The Men's Chorus. They sang a few simple folk songs and, because it was a demonstration concert even consented to show the audience some of the warm-up exercises and activities that we used on a daily basis in rehearsal. When we were done you would have thought the late Pavarotti just finished an aria by the way the audience affirmed these young men with their applause. Needless to say, the initial mountain had been scaled and while it was always a challenging group to conduct, the rest of the year went much more smoothly because trust had been established and the bar had been set: they had met the expectations set before them—expectations that were finally high enough to do justice to them as individuals and to the experience of music making itself—and were ready to move to the next level.

Our ability to persuade and motivate musicians is directly connected to the kinds of expectations we set. Don't limit the ensemble by assuming they can't achieve. Resist the temptation to categorize an ensemble if by doing so this means limiting them. "They're only freshmen" (or only a church choir). "We only meet twice a week" (or for a 25-minute period). "They're professionals (or college students); they want to do it their way." These kinds of statements limit our musicians before we even begin. When we lead, it is our job to inspire the ensemble to reach not for perfection but for excellence. Leading means persuading musicians to reach for the next level, not because they have to or *else* (coercion) but because they *can*.

> Successful leaders have high expectations, both of themselves and of their constituents. These expectations are powerful because they are the frames into which people fit reality. People are much more likely to see what they expect to see even when it differs from what may be actually occurring…. If we expect others to fail, they probably will. If we expect them to succeed, they probably will.[91]

Set a high bar. Even if you don't reach it, at least you have moved upward. Don't use fear to motivate; use promise and potential

---

91   Kouzes and Posner, 321–2.

to inspire. Find ways to paint a picture of possibility for the ensemble that will be compelling for them. Everyone wants to be excellent and it is much easier to have an effective rehearsal if musicians see their time and efforts bringing them toward something valid and worth accomplishing.

ESTABLISH A CULTURE OF DISCIPLINE

When I read Jim Collins' *Good to Great* I was struck by what he describes as a "culture of discipline." Despite the images the phrase might suggest, a culture of discipline it is not a tyrannical regime or a strict system with no room for freedom. A culture of discipline involves two key elements: a highly developed *system* of operation that allows for freedom and responsibility and *people* who are self-disciplined.

Much of what we have already discussed in this book addresses the first part of this formula. A highly developed system of operation depends on your vision, organizational and administrative skills, your preparation and planning and constant reevaluation to make improvements. In Chapter Four we examined how we can lead our rehearsals so that musicians have more freedom within this operation—freedom to make suggestions, even decisions regarding the music and other aspects related to the organization—and to develop a sense of responsibility or ownership for the musical work of the ensemble.

More important and more challenging to accomplish is the second part of the culture of discipline formula: having people in the organization who themselves are disciplined in thought and action. Ideally, in building a great organization one begins with self-disciplined people. Collins uses the metaphor of "getting the right people on the bus" or in our case in the ensemble or on the board. A culture of discipline depends on individuals who have a high degree of personal discipline who do not need to be managed but who manage themselves. These are the musicians who assume they need to work on their music outside of rehearsal or board members who accomplish administrative tasks with little supervision and who initiate activities that they see a need for, all to be sure the work of the ensemble happens smoothly. Having self-disciplined people in our ensembles and other places in our organizations allows us to manage the system and lead the people rather than manage both the system and the people.

The reality is, however, that we do not always have control over who is in our ensembles; we don't always have the luxury of selecting only the highly disciplined to play or sing with us. If we are lucky we have at least one auditioned group in our organization—and then the bus metaphor may apply—but what about the many ensembles we direct that are open to everyone in the school, community or church? Can we establish a culture of discipline with a kaleidoscope of personal agendas and work ethics? Can we persuade others to think and act as self-disciplined members of the ensemble?

Yes, at least for the majority of the musicians we lead. Our teaching, our vision, our leadership and our modeling can grow others, not just in terms of their musical skill but also in terms of who they become as people—and that means people willing to take owner-ship of themselves and the organization. *People grow in self discipline when they are excited about their experience, when they believe they are contributing to it in a significant way and when they can envision the end result as highly successful.* These are the ingredients of intrinsic motivation, another way of describing self-discipline and something we spend a lot of time wondering how to grow among our musicians. When we create an ensemble or organization that allows people to meet these needs they become, in large percentages, self-disciplined and you are free to be a leader.

Establishing a culture of discipline is not only important for the ensemble now; it is just as important for the ensemble when we leave the organization. If the ensemble is only successful because of our discipline, our sheer force of will, then when that force is gone the organization falters. In companies where this was the case

Collins found "a spectacular rise under a tyrannical disciplinarian, followed by an equally spectacular decline when the disciplinarian stepped away, leaving behind no enduring culture of discipline...."[92] A great leader leaves a legacy not only by what he creates when he is in a position of power but by what endures when he leaves the organization. Strive to create a culture of discipline now and for the future.

REFUSE THE TALENT TANGLE

The Talent Tangle is my name for the power struggle we engage in with musicians that push us to our limits of patience and integrity by manipulating the situation, other musicians and very often, us.

You know the musicians I am talking about: they are bright, talented, usually people-savvy and very capable of turning on and off emotions, facial expressions and personas. They are the musicians who, for one reason or another, want to control the situation; they know they are musically valuable to the ensemble and are going to take advantage of the situation by trying to control us and everything related to the organization. They show up late or miss rehearsal, knowing that "we can't do without them" and believing they won't be reprimanded, fired or replaced. They always know when we make a mistake or miss a cue and think nothing of letting us—and everyone else in the ensemble—know about it. They work behind our backs to spread rumors, negatively influence others' thinking and generally raise doubt and questions about who we are and what we do. In short, they make our lives as leaders even more complicated than they already are and they challenge our patience, our tongues and our character.

So what do we do? How do we handle musicians like these, especially when they really *do* play an important role in the musical end result?

---

92 Collins, 133.

First ask yourself what is at the root of their attitude. While conductors are not typically also licensed psychologists, we do come to learn much about human behavior and motivation by working with every type of musician personality over time. Usually you will encounter two broad categories of Talent Tanglers. The first is the musician who is not really a bad person but has, at least in his or her mind, been offended, hurt or simply not encouraged or acknowledged. For this Tangler, taking the time to give them what they need can usually put things right and often turns a negative personality into a strong leader and advocate for the ensemble. In other words, taking the time to talk to this musician or to assess what they need and provide it, whether it is an apology, an authentic word of encouragement or a task that demonstrates our confidence in their ability can work wonders for the situation. I can think of so many individuals with whom I have worked who fall into this category and virtually all of them turned into huge success stories.

The second category of Tanglers is much more troublesome. These are the musicians who have deep, unmet needs that have nothing to do with the organization or us. They have psychological or emotional baggage that disturbs every area of their lives, including, unfortunately, the part they share with us. They may be on medication or in therapy—or need to be, but aren't yet—or they may be dealing with passive/aggressive behavior, a huge lack of self-esteem or deep-seated anger or resentment (at a parent, a spouse, a sibling—you name it). When we step back and realize that this is the cause of their inappropriate actions with us and with the ensemble it helps us to understand, even sympathize—but it is important not to allow our feelings of pity or empathy to blind us to the need to take action. Certainly we should do whatever we can to be sure this musician gets the help they need and especially if we are working in a public school there are procedures for handling confidential information that may be shared with us and for referring these individuals to the appropriate professional for help. But we also have a responsibility to everyone else in the ensemble, a responsibility to protect their experience and to ensure a safe and reasonable working environment. If we just look the other way, shaking our heads or worse yet, tangling with this talent—arguing, trading sarcastic comments, pulling rank—we only add to the problem.

I'll never forget being in an undergraduate methods course when the professor cooked up a scheme to engage in a verbal battle with two star students in front of the class just to demonstrate what *not* to do. Even though we were told after the fact that it was just a demonstration, the emotions I felt in witnessing that public conflict stayed with me long beyond that day's class. As an onlooker to a tangle between the authority figure and two of my classmates I was emotionally churned up and it really colored my feelings for the learning environment that were never the same after that.

That is the experience we create when we publicly tangle with a member of the ensemble. We must avoid this at all costs. Start by assessing the situation and talking in person and in private with the Tangler. Tell him you are aware he is unhappy or dissatisfied and give him the opportunity to tell you why. Do not allow him to brush it off and leave without making clear that you are sincerely interested in his experience but just as interested and committed to the experience of *everyone* in the ensemble. And because you are committed to that you will not let his behavior continue because it is having negative effects. Decide in advance what the consequences will be if he does not change. It may be a lowered grade, removal from the ensemble, a meeting with the pastor or being let go from his contract depending on the situation and setting. But be sure you are clear and you stick to your word or you will only exacerbate the problem and it will spread.

In our field, talent and strong egos go hand in hand. You may have convinced yourself that this is just part of the business and you have little control over it. I challenge you to raise your standards and believe that there are other musicians out there or other avenues to take. *You do not have to be a slave to talent*; the quality of the experience and the environment in which you and the ensemble work together is under your direct control, ultimately, so take responsibility as a leader and take action.

Perhaps one final story will illustrate this point. I know of a theatrical director who was working with an actor who had the lead in a play but who took advantage of his role by coming late to rehearsals, acting rudely to other actors and generally abusing all privileges. Despite being talked to, this actor continued to think he was untouchable and so he pushed even further by coming seriously late to call on opening night. He obviously thought "After all, what can the director do? I'm the lead; they can't do the show without me."

Oh, yeah? By the time Mr. Talent Tangler walked in the director had already taken action by filtering in a talented though unrehearsed actor from the second act to take the place of this egomaniac (who fortunately only appeared in the first act). The replacement walked through approximate staging minutes before curtain and during the show took cues from the director who laid on the floor behind the couch, out of sight from the audience, and fed lines as necessary. I was in the audience that night and can tell you I never enjoyed a performance more. The audience was only told there had to be a last minute substitution and not only accepted it but applauded everyone's efforts. Truthfully, the script was funnier and more interesting with the change in actors!

It may not be so easy in your situation. You may conduct a professional ensemble complicated with unions, contracts and long-standing reputations and relationships. You might be tangling with a student whose ethnicity may make taking action look like an act of discrimination. I don't know what your situation is or what the nature of your tangle may be but I am convinced there is always an alternative, if not as dramatic as the one above which preserves the experience and the performance. At the least, if you have to endure finishing a performance with a Tangler, make changes before the next rehearsal cycle or concert so you do not have to go through this again—at least, not with the same Tangler. If you do not you may find that you lose other excellent performers and people in the ensemble with great attitudes and spirits who simply do not want to stay around and endure any more of the drama.

> Letting the wrong people hang around is unfair to all the right people, as they inevitably find themselves compensating for the inadequacies of the wrong people. Worse, it can drive away the best people. Strong performers are intrinsically motivated by performance, and when they see their efforts impeded by carrying extra weight, they eventually become frustrated.[93]

PERSUASION—THE BOTTOM LINE

As conductors we must *move* people: to convince them, to make them believe in us and in themselves, in the music and in our joint musical goals. We need to be masters of persuasion, but *how* we persuade reveals everything about our commitment to leadership. Frankly, coercion is easier. We can pull rank, hide behind our authority or elaborate rules systems and make it happen pronto. Reality tells us that sometimes we need to use strong tactics; when the stakes are high, when time is tight, then we better remember who is the leader and we had better take charge.

But—

These instances will be few and far between if we personally commit to becoming better leaders. If we plan, prepare, build trust relationships, treat people as more than enactors of sound, keep our ego in check and make decisions that are not based on our own self-edification then we are growing into principle-centered servant leaders. And that means we are developing a way of operating that will not

---

93   Collins, 56.

demand as many crunch situations which call for strong tactics. When we *do* have to display our authority people will respect it because they realize it was necessary. We will have earned the honor and reputation necessary so that our actions are seen not as self-motivated but rather as the best decision under the circumstances. And even when it was not—when we were coercive just because it was our human nature under pressure—the residue of that action will not be nearly as damaging or lingering because we have built a strong foundation with the ensemble.

Persuasion starts with knowing what you are about, knowing where your ensemble is headed, believing in yourself and your musicians and not allowing setbacks to discourage you. *The authentic and consistent strength of your convictions will persuade others to join you.*

In the early stages of your work as a conductor (either your early career or your first weeks with a new ensemble), simple motivators or rewards are often effective. We have all relied on the power of free food (donuts and coffee for my 7:00 AM college men's chorus) or other reward systems to help nudge musicians to come to rehearsal, learn their music, memorize their words or whatever else is on your agenda. But as you build a foundation of something more intrinsically rewarding, those simple motivators are no longer necessary (though you may keep them for fun). *Excellence is the ultimate persuader.* Don't spend so much time on the campaign—the frills, the incentives, the packaging—that you find the actual product isn't worth anything on its own. Be excellent, model excellence and teach for excellence and you will be rewarded with excellence.

Persuasion only works when you connect with people, and a large part of that depends on your ability to understand life from their perspective. Talking to a junior high student means knowing what is important to him, what matters in his world and what interests or annoys him. When you have a sense of these things you are more likely to be listened to and it is more likely that your ideas will be given a chance. But the same can be said about working with a professional cellist. Knowing what is important to her, what matters in her world and what interests or annoys her will be critical if you are going to have any hope of getting her on board with your ideas. "Whether you are selling a product, service, or an idea, it always pays to remember that the person you are trying to convince always wants to know, What's in it for me? You'll never convince anyone verbally until you answer that question."[94] Or put another way:

> People must believe that leaders understand their needs and have their interests at heart. Leadership is a dialogue, not a monologue. To enlist support, leaders must have intimate knowledge of people's dreams, hopes, aspirations, visions, and values.[95]

Human nature always needs a nudge. Even the most disciplined musicians get discouraged, tired or unfocused from time to time. Provide that nudge. Remind them of why they are there, the opportunity they have to create something of great value, the chance to contribute in their unique way and the opportunity they have to grow and become even better at what they do. Generate new ideas and be open to theirs so you always have something to look forward to—a new place to go, artistically speaking.

I wrote an article a few years back about rehearsal design and techniques that I entitled "Invite, Instruct, and Inspire."[96] Those three words sum up what we do as conductors if we are using persuasion as our modus operandi. Rather than "coerce, drill, and punish," conductor-leaders *invite* their musicians into the process, *instruct* them so they have the skills, knowledge, and understanding they need and *inspire* them to be the best ensemble they can be. That is the bottom line.

---

94   Mills, 88.
95   Kouzes and Posner, 15.
96   Ramona M. Wis, "Invite, Instruct, and Inspire: Techniques for the Choral Rehearsal" (*Teaching Music*, 1998).

Responsibility and Tough Decisions

This chapter has been about the wise use of power: specifically, the call to use a persuasive approach generated by our passion and our ability to paint a clear picture of the end goal rather than a coercive approach relying on authority and intimidation hidden behind the accepted mantle of artistic temperament. Throughout this book we have attempted to illustrate a way of leading that is people-centered, positive, collaborative and aimed at excellence in artistry. All are good things. But even the best, most respected leaders face situations and encounter people that don't neatly respond to their efforts. Does that make everything we have talked about pie-in-the-sky idealism?

No. The values remain constant, even when—especially when—challenges arise. Holding a contract over the head of a less-than-responsible singer can be a coercive tactic or it may be simply the right leadership choice. If you have no ability to understand and interact with people in a respectful manner, if you have not set clear expectations and not kept your part of the bargain by being less than prepared or skilled at your job or if you are a reactive personality that immediately wants to fix uncomfortable situations by shutting down others, then you will use tactics like "I can fire you" as your primary mode of operating. If on the other hand you have laid all the groundwork for great relationships and a great musical experience and a musician still does not hold up her end of the bargain, then it is your responsibility as the leader to be sure the integrity of the ensemble and all the individuals in the organization are maintained, in which case, saying "You have a contract and need to fulfill it or you will be let go" is the only wise leadership choice.

There *will* be conflicts and uncooperative musicians. But as you become a better leader and as you develop a better ensemble built on enduring principles you should encounter fewer conflicts and less resistance. In other words, since there are no perfect people there are no perfect leaders and no perfect ensembles. There are, however, great ensembles with talented, wise, effective conductors who understand how to balance the elements of vision, trust, teaching and persuasion in order for the best possible experience and highest quality performance. The rewards are great for those principle-centered servant leaders Covey talks about, for the leaders we can become:

> As their understanding of the relationship between power and leadership increases, their ability to lead others and to have influence with others without forcing them will grow. And they may experience an unusual peace of mind that comes with being a wiser, more effective leader.[97]

---

97   Covey, 108.

THE BULLY SEED ⁓

Every parent has seen some form of bullying take place in their own child's experience, whether through overt behavior (I am thinking of one particularly nasty day on the playground after school) or more subtle forms of intimidation. I remember my daughter's early days in middle school when she had a locker neighbor who would routinely open her own door so wide that my daughter couldn't open hers; who stood just enough over to her side that my daughter had no room—and no time—to get in and out of her locker during those all-too-short passing periods, causing her frustration and embarrassment at being late to class. Because it happened regularly and with an attitude of purposefulness it was clear this girl enjoyed the control she had in this situation, exerting a form of power over my daughter. While my daughter eventually found ways to work through and resolve the situation, it got me thinking about what kinds of adults kids like this turn out to be. What does this way of dealing with people look like 10, 20, 30 years later?

Kids will be kids. Junior high students are hormonal. High schoolers are just trying to fit in. College students are finding their own way. We excuse behavior with clichés like these, throwing our hands up in apparent helplessness and with a blind eye to what this seemingly normal behavior can become. But when we accept coercive behavior at any age and in any form we allow the seed to grow. I have a colleague who, by his condescending tone and body language, his rolling eyes and his negative attitude could intimidate

Donald Trump. And I know of many conductors whose coercive rehearsal tactics are the grown up equivalent of name-calling and peer pressure. Were these the bullies, or maybe the victims of bullying when they were middle school kids?

Coercion exists in many forms and in every aspect of life, from the salesperson who pressures us to the department chair who makes it uncomfortable to say "no" to yet another administrative task. While we can't change everyone else, we can refuse to use these tactics in our own work; and with those we lead we can use our influence to show a better way of moving people to action. Do not allow subtle demonstrations of coercion to go unchecked when you see them in your musicians, students, co-workers—wherever you have influence—or you will allow the seed to grow. Take these opportunities as teaching moments or mentoring opportunities. Find ways to help others examine their approach and then share some alternative methods. You will uncover the reasons for their actions and hopefully you will be a model they can look to when trying to learn another way.

CHAPTER SIX

LEAD WITH CHARACTER ~

*What you are shouts so loud in my ears I cannot
hear what you say.*
—Ralph Waldo Emerson

When I was in my early thirties I was widowed very suddenly.
In the midst of trying to cope with the emotional loss and all the
adjustments one would expect under the circumstances I also found
myself stepping into the job my late husband had at the time of
his death, that of entertainment director of a professional dinner
theatre. I had been involved on the staff and as a cast member of
the theatre but had been able to remain more on the artistic side of
operations. I had not had to concern myself with issues of marketing,
management, producers and the almighty financial bottom line.
That is, until I became the director.

The cast and the rest of the staff were terrific; they stepped
into additional roles to ensure that the show already running would
continue to run smoothly and that the show in rehearsal could open
on time and of a quality that would equal or surpass the current
show. Unfortunately, this optimism and faith were not fully shared
by my boss, the producer and general manager of the resort in
which this theatre was housed.

Just a few days before the show opened the producer came to watch rehearsal. Everything was going well; we were positioned to open very strongly. However, the producer got cold feet and started thinking that there were too many numbers involving the singing waiters, waitresses and the featured quartet. He thought the show's headliners (a dubious title for two impersonator/comedians with only some voiceover and cable TV work behind them) should be on stage almost all the time—and so he decided we should cut eleven numbers from the show. *Eleven.* It didn't take a genius to figure out that the majority of the cast, people who had given up their entire summer and consented to wait tables just so they could be featured in a few numbers, would not be performing at all.

Talk about a nightmare. As you would expect, several people went up to the dressing room and began packing up their belongings. They were no longer performers who waited tables; they were waiters, period. Why should they stick around? They had passed up other opportunities to perform that summer but had chosen this theatre because they banked on the reputation of the director, now deceased, and the excellent staff and cast that he always attracted. Even after his death the cast had honored their commitment and even stepped it up to ensure the success of the operation; and now this.

As the leader of this enterprise, I diplomatically tried to persuade the producer to change his mind on artistic grounds. I talked about the show's balance and variety, the need to maintain the logistical flow and the quality of the numbers he proposed cutting. But nothing I said mattered. I was talking to a wall; art and people were the least of his concerns. He wanted to be sure he would have a profitable bottom line and he was convinced that the show as originally designed wouldn't net the profit.

"But it's not right." Silence; a cold stare. I had finally told the producer what I really believed—that it was not right, not ethical, to renege on the promise we had made to these people. I knew the sacrifices they had made and I had faith in their abilities and a

strong vision for the quality of the show. I was willing to risk my position there for the cast who had been working tirelessly, pushing themselves, and who had been loyal to the theatre and to me.

There must have been something in the strength of my convictions and the way in which I presented them because the producer conceded—though not without a long, cold look into my eyes and a promise to pull the plug on the whole thing if it didn't work out as I had envisioned. I'll never forget that moment as long as I live, nor the moments that followed: my running out to the parking lot to catch people before they quit and telling them we were still on; holding my breath during previews, attended by the press; reading the reviews that gave the show a thumbs-up and breathing a sigh of relief when the producer said we could continue the show as originally designed for the full run.

I've come to think of that experience as a moment of truth for me. I'm not quite sure where the courage came from for me to stand up to the producer, a man who was very intimidating and who could have fired me on the spot. And I remember not thinking about what I was doing as some kind of power play or heroic feat; I just knew that what he wanted to do *wasn't right*, ethically or artistically. My integrity wouldn't allow it and I had to let him know, even if it meant I would be walking out to the parking lot along with the rest of the cast. The good news, of course, is that everything turned out fine; the show was a success and life went on. But I've come to believe that even if things don't turn out to be successful, on whatever terms you use to measure success, choosing character and integrity always means you choose right.

CHARACTER AND LEADERSHIP

At the foundation of everything we have talked about in this book—vision, trust, teaching, persuasion and all aspects of these leadership areas—is character. Our character is the source for our actions, our relationships and our understanding. Character is not something we turn on and off. Character is who we are deep down under all the layers of training and experience, all the professional titles and accomplishments and all the quirks or charms of personality. It is just as much who we are when nobody's looking[98] as who we are when everybody's looking.

> As much as we try to separate the leader from the person, the two are totally inseparable. Unfortunately, many people tend to split off the *act of leadership* from the person. We tend to view leadership as an external event. We see it only as something people do.... Leadership is not simply something we do. It comes from somewhere inside us. Leadership is a process, an intimate expression of who we are. It is our being in action. Our being, our personhood, says as much about us as a leader as the act of leading itself.[99]

Character is always reflected in our leadership and it marks the difference between those who are leaders in title and authority only and those who are real, authentic, even great leaders. Character is everything we are that we bring to the podium. It is our heart in action, our wisdom displayed and our strength tested.

If I think of character from the ensemble's point of view, it seems to me that more than almost anyone else the conductor on the podium is the person whom I want to know has a strong, authentic and admirable character. This is the person who is going to enter into, even control, my musical space, who is going to call on me to express myself deeply and who is going to guide me through difficult challenges. Do I want to give that responsibility over to someone whom I cannot respect, whose character is questionable and whose

---

98 I recommend reading Bill Hybels' book *Character: Who You Are When No One's Looking*, Downers Grove, IL: InterVarsity Press, 1987.

99 Cashman, 18.

response to adversity is to bail out or use dehumanizing tactics? Do we really believe character is separate from musical competency and leadership?

Character is everything. In this final chapter I will call us to examine the relationship of character to our leadership role as conductors and to look at aspects of who we are, on and off the podium, in an attempt to help us round out our understanding of what is means to be an authentic, successful, conductor-leader. We will look at developing our character, linking our character and actions in a more congruent way and protecting and strengthening ourselves so that our character can continue to remain strong.

KEYS TO CHARACTER
BE THE SAME PERSON ON AND OFF THE PODIUM—
BE AUTHENTIC

In Chapter Three we talked about the need for us to be consistent in our daily behavior and decisions if we are to be deemed trustworthy by those we lead: being consistent in what we do. Closely related to this is the notion of integrity or of being consistent in *who we are* both on and off the podium.

Having integrity means being integrated, being whole; connecting all parts of ourselves into one person. Though we may express ourselves in different ways when we are on the podium (more animated, more overt) than when we are off (perhaps quiet and more of a listener in social settings), the same set of values and beliefs should underpin both of these dimensions of who we are. "When I have integrity, my words and my deeds match up. I am who I am, no matter where I am or who I am with."[100]

Being the same person on and off the podium does not mean wearing your heart on your sleeve, revealing your deep, dark secrets

---

100 John C. Maxwell, *Developing the Leader Within You*, Nashville: Thomas Nelson Publishers, 1993, 35.

and the intimate parts of your personal and family life. Frankly, that's no one's business and it has no place in the rehearsal. While an occasional example or story from one's life, shared in a heartfelt or humorous manner can be an effective and endearing connection between conductor and ensemble, people expect and respect the line between professional and personal life.

Being authentic means being guided by a core set of values and beliefs and working to express these values consistently whether at home, in a rehearsal, at church or at a board meeting. It is being a whole person and sharing that person in various ways and in the multiple settings that make up our lives. Without this consistency and without a core set of values, our character is questionable because it is unclear—even to ourselves—who we really are.

Imagine this scenario: A mentor of yours, someone whom you greatly respect for his artistry or talents in another field as well as his leadership expertise meets you for lunch at a local restaurant. Throughout the meal and your conversation about important life questions your mentor routinely criticizes the waiter, even to the point of acting superior and condescending towards him for minor annoyances like forgetting to refill the water glass. Your mentor is brusque, even rude, and decides to deliver a short lecture to the waiter on the subject of how he should do his job.

How would you feel about your mentor after this experience? Would you simply dismiss the event as typical (you know, you just can't get good help these days), choosing to make no connection between your mentor's behavior towards this waiter and his professional persona? Or would you wonder about the heart of a person that was so quick to judge others and so in need of boosting his own status in the pettiest of ways? Once you witnessed this split personality, would you have the same level of trust or would you find yourself struggling to tell the difference between the person and the image?

> If I try to use human influence strategies and tactics of how to get other people to do what I want, to work better, to be more motivated, to like me and each other—while my character is fundamentally flawed, marked by duplicity and insincerity—then, in the long run, I cannot be successful. My duplicity will breed distrust, and everything I do—even using so-called good human relations techniques—will be perceived as manipulative.[101]

Of course, we all have bad days—no one is perfect, so we will occasionally lose it and act less than graciously. But the authentic person, the person whom we say has integrity would ultimately do something to right that wrong, whether it meant apologizing to the waiter or at the very least, to you, acknowledging his shortcomings and your discomfort and embarrassment in witnessing them. Remember, leadership does not mean perfection but rather a commitment to excellence whether as an artist or as a person. Failures along the way do not derail authentic leaders; they simply act as corrections and guides to something better—they are opportunities to learn and grow, to do things better next time.

Authenticity means realizing that we are one person who may express herself in multiple ways all stemming from the same core. Like a tree trunk, the core is strong and serves as the foundation for the limbs of our lives—conductor, teacher, spouse, parent, church and community member, friend. For each of the limbs to grow and be healthy, to prosper and be successful, the core must be strong and firm. As conductors that strength of character can only help us to lead more effectively and to earn the legitimate power Covey talks of because we will be honored by the musicians we lead.

---

101 Stephen R. Covey, *The 7 Seven Habits of Highly Effective People* (New York: Simon & Schuster, 1989), 21.

Can we continue to keep a split personality working for us, acting as a conductor who does and says all the right things and gets a respectable artistic product but is really a person with an incongruous or questionable character? As with all masquerades, the charade must eventually come to an end. At some point we are revealed for who we are—apart from what we are and what we have done.

DEVELOP A PERSONAL MISSION STATEMENT

There has been a big move in recent years towards companies or organizations, including musical organizations or academic institutions, writing mission statements. These can range from short statements of purpose to longer statements expressing vision or values. More and more, people are also writing individual or personal mission statements—a powerful exercise, and I believe a critical starting place for any professional endeavor. It is also a revealing exercise, one which forces you to reflect upon your gifts, your passions and your core values and one which will go a long way toward helping you understand who you are—necessary if you are going to become an integrated person.

The skeptic in you may be thinking "Oh no, another touchy-feely exercise that will take a lot of time and result in a piece of paper that collects dust somewhere." Unfortunately, this can be true if you don't understand how a personal mission statement can work for you. A mission statement is a tool, a compass that can help you make decisions that are in line with your values, help you stay on track towards the most important, broader life goals you have set for yourself and help you stay away from "opportunities" that may in fact be distractions or worse, derailments from your purpose.

A mission statement answers the questions "What am I here for?" "How can I uniquely contribute?" "What is my role in my many spheres of influence?" "What are my gifts?" It keeps you above the small, task-oriented, nitty-gritty details most of us obsess over every day and allows you to hover over life at a higher level where the view is much broader and clearer when it comes to seeing what is really important and what our unique, individual contribution can be.

Crafting a mission statement begins by thinking about your unique gifts or talents. Don't limit yourself to thinking that talents are necessarily defined by career fields (like conducting, or even music). Think at a broader level: do you have an uncanny ability to seek out and work with detail? Do you have a unique aesthetic sensibility, the gift of discerning gradations in sound and color? Do you have a knack for working with people, for understanding and handling a variety of personality types and for being able to move them to action? Maybe you have a talent for making complicated ideas seem simple or a gift for organization.

Because our gifts are so much a part of who we are we can have trouble recognizing them as gifts—it's just what we do naturally, nothing special. Asking others for input, those who know us well and whom we trust is a wise move. Ask friends or colleagues what they find unique about you, what appears to come more naturally to you than to others. I can think of three distinct conversations in the past ten years that had a big impact on my coming to understand my own gifts. One, with my friend and colleague Judy on a flight to a music convention in which she told me I was so good at understanding, analyzing and talking to others about process, as in the process of teaching or leading or conducting. The second, a conversation with a friend from my church, Celia, who had worked with me on the music team and who gratefully observed that I had the gift of encouragement. The third from my colleague Jack, centered on my public speaking gifts: "Man, you could do this for a living!" Hearing these assessments from others whose opinions I valued, I immediately recognized them as true yet I am not sure I would have been able to see these traits in myself without the insight of these friends and colleagues.

Once you have determined your gifts, reflect on your passions, the activities that you love to do and that seem to energize you rather than drain you. What can you do for hours without stopping to eat or without checking the clock? What makes you excited about getting out of bed in the morning? What makes you genuinely happy? It may surprise you that the act of conducting is not at the top of your list. Perhaps, despite the fact that you work with large groups of people, you really get into flow[102] when you are alone, researching intently at your computer or when you are sitting on the other side of the podium, attending to your own music making instead of thinking on behalf of all the members of the ensemble. Maybe you are fascinated by the challenge of administrating a program such as an academic department or love helping people understand complexities that you break down for them. Discovering these things about yourself doesn't necessarily mean you need to resign from your conducting position tomorrow but it can help you think about whether you are *using your gifts in the best way* and can help you consider fine-tuning your career as you frame the rest of your life.

Finally, when you come to understand your unique gifts and acknowledge your passions, reflect on your core values or deepest beliefs and how these interface with one another. This is an important step in the process if we are to lead congruent lives where deep beliefs and outward behavior match up in a seamless, natural way. Often our frustration as professionals comes from living with a constant internal struggle—being, wanting one way on the inside and doing, acting a different way on the outside. Until we reconcile these differences, we will never be happy, personally or professionally. What really matters to you? What are those non-negotiables in your thinking that, when threatened cause you to feel out of balance?

---

102 To learn more about this state of flow read Mihaly Csikszentmihaly's book *Flow: The Psychology of Optimal Experience* (New York: Harper and Row, 1990).

Armed with an understanding of your gifts, passions and core values, you can begin to put into words what you believe your mission to be. I wrote my own personal mission statement about five years ago when I was teaching a course for women leaders through the college's Entrepreneurship Institute. After working with the women for a short time and sensing their need to get centered in order to make decisions about the next step in each of their lives, I decided to assign them the task of writing a personal mission statement to be brought to class the following week. Though I was sure I already had myself figured out pretty well, I thought I had better complete the assignment myself in order to have an actual written statement which I could present to the class (I should take my own advice). What I discovered was that writing a personal mission statement was a completely revealing and freeing exercise. Here is what I came to understand as my unique mission:

> *My mission is to use my God-given talents and oppor-*
> *tunities to improve the lives of all those I come in contact*
> *with. Through my actions, my passion and my ability to*
> *teach and lead, I want to help move people forward to a*
> *better, more fulfilling and more deeply enriched life. I want*
> *to help others learn how to create this life for themselves and*
> *for those they reach so they can extend their own influence*
> *in a never-ending chain.*

Notice that there is nothing in this statement specifically about music or conducting or how well my ensemble will sing. What is evident is my understanding of my leadership and teaching gifts, my passion for people and desire to help them grow and have a richer life and my core belief that these gifts are not mine but are given to me to use by God. Your statement will be just as personal, just as reflective of your values whatever those may be. If it is really well thought out, your mission statement will relate equally well to your family life, your professional life and your spiritual life and will guide your thinking and action as you move more specifically into your work as a conductor.

Take the time to write your personal mission statement without worrying about how it sounds, whether it is corny or correct or whether others will agree with it. Go back to your statement from time to time and see whether anything in it needs to be revised, refined or drastically changed. Most of all, keep it available for you to reference, especially during those times when you are struggling with a decision or trying to gain some clarity during a particularly turbulent time. Let your mission statement be your compass.

MAKE DECISIONS BASED ON YOUR VALUES

The underlying theme of this chapter is knowing your deep values and acting on them in a consistent manner in all aspects of your life. As director of the theatre I made a decision to act based on my values, even at the risk of losing my job and professional reputation. Nobody would have blamed me if I had rationalized that this was professional theatre, that it was a job and had nothing to do with my personal beliefs. After all, that is what we are told about the way to do business.

When we get into this mindset we lose our nerve, maintain the status quo and a part of us dies, I think, because we lose hope that any real, positive change in this world is possible. We think, sure, it would be nice if human qualities could have a place in our professional lives, but that's not possible so we just do what we have always done, follow everyone else's lead and believe what we have been told about the way it is.

But if, instead, we make decisions based on our values we do two things: we *strengthen our character* because we act with integrity and we *make decisions that are more likely to be good ones for us, professionally and personally* because they are grounded in our core beliefs.

Instead of being swayed by public opinion or even the vanity of our own ego wanting to take every opportunity that comes our way, we assess the situation against our values and see if the two mesh.

About two years ago I was offered the position of Artistic Director/Conductor of a Chicago-area professional chorus. As I went through all the stages of the interview, including a conducting audition/rehearsal and discussions with various people involved in the organization I shared an exciting vision for the organization: how it could develop musically, how it could grow audiences and its reputation and what role it could ultimately play in the profession. It was an exciting process and, I must admit one that was good for my ego, as I received several acknowledgements along the way and affirmations of my ability and previously established reputation in the choral field. In other words, it felt great to be wanted.

But when it came down to making the final decision I had a long heart-to-heart talk with myself to assess the opportunity on every level, including the level of my deep values. What I came to realize was that taking on this position in addition to my already demanding roles at the college and my responsibilities to my family would mean putting a strain on everyone to whom I was already obligated, not to mention my own health and well-being. This position was not just one of conducting the ensemble but would mean doing everything I have talked about in this book: establishing a trust relationship with the singers as well as the board (the easier part); being patient about making certain changes despite a strong vision (the harder part); and teaching everyone in the organization a different way to handle operations from rehearsals to marketing to program design (not easy or hard, just work). If I were going to do this job properly I would want to do it in a values-oriented way; but to do that would take time and energy that meant compromising my work and relationships in other areas.

I turned the job down.

Strangely (or so it seemed to me at the time), once I made this decision I did not feel a sense of regret over a lost opportunity. As a matter of fact, there was a kind of inner confirmation, a calm that I felt almost immediately. The next day, when I shared this whole process with my friend Ari, a fine conductor and professional life coach, she didn't make a judgment about whether I had made a good or bad decision; she did, however, very enthusiastically acknowledge that what I had done was make a decision based on my *values*—and that was a very good thing indeed.

I also believed that if it was meant to be, this kind of opportunity would come around again, either when my life and responsibilities could better accommodate it or when the position itself was changed. About three months after the job was originally offered to me I received an email from one of the board members telling me that the ensemble had, for a number of reasons disbanded and reorganized itself. They were planning to perform their inaugural season under guest conductors—conductors who would have little administrative responsibility and a condensed schedule of rehearsals and performance—and they expressed their desire for me to conduct the first concert of this new professional chorus. With its reconfigured schedule and responsibilities the position was now do-able for me so I heartily accepted their offer. By making decisions based on my values I wound up with a much better scenario, one that fit with my life and other responsibilities much better. My values had guided me both times so both decisions were right for me.

BE RIGOROUS WITH YOURSELF FIRST

Rigor can be defined as "the application of precise and exacting standards in the doing of something." Conductors can be rigorous in their work with ensembles—drilling for precision in playing or singing, holding the musicians to high standards of musical expression and demanding promptness so that rehearsals start on time. Rigor is necessary for any individual or organization hoping to achieve greatness and is often used as a tool of assessment: the demonstrated level of rigor in an academic course at the college, for example, is a key element in determining a faculty member's effectiveness in the classroom.

One of a leader's tests of character is how well she uses rigor in the organization. Certainly conductors would want to apply precise and exacting standards to the music the ensemble performs and to the way rehearsals and the entire organization is run; but rigor must start with the conductor's approach to his or her own development, preparation, attitude and professionalism.

When things are going poorly, weak or inconsistent leaders will attempt to disguise their own failings by lashing out at others around them, firing people (or replacing them in the ensemble), blaming them for lack of preparation or just expecting more from them than is reasonable. What these leaders try to call rigor really turns into ruthlessness as they take almost any action in an attempt to salvage the sinking ship that was their responsibility to steer.

Character means looking inward first and holding oneself to high standards before expecting others to reach those standards. When you come to rehearsal unprepared, when your musicianship atrophies due to lack of regular exercise, when you fail to meet commitments or are an organizational mess, you model a lack of rigor for every musician in the room and make it difficult if not impossible to hold them to high standards. "Rigor...applies first at the top, focused on those who hold the largest burden of responsibility."[103] Rigor must be applied inwardly before it can be mandated outwardly if conductors are to be authentic leaders. It is another challenge and responsibility of leadership but a necessary one if we are to be respected by the ensemble and if we are to know, in our own minds and hearts that we are who we pretend to be.

---

103   Collins, 53.

BALANCE PROFESSIONAL GOALS
WITH THE REST OF YOUR LIFE

Those who know me would not be surprised to find out I own lots of motivational books and CDs that deal with setting professional goals. I am by nature a goal-oriented person and depend on goals to keep me motivated and interested in virtually every aspect of my life. Goals give me a sense of direction, a feeling of renewal and help me to feel I am moving forward as I grow in multiple ways.

But it is all too easy to focus the majority of our energies on professional goals to the point of neglecting the rest of our life— our family, friends, community, spiritual life or personal health and well-being. Conducting, regardless of the level of the ensemble can be an all-consuming job, not just in terms of the actual time it takes to prepare and lead rehearsals and conduct performances but in the constant mind energy it takes as we work out creative problems—of which there is never a shortage. Because we spend our energy this way, we are much more likely to be able to articulate where the orchestra is headed in the next five years than where our family or our exercise regimen will be in the next week.

You may be very uncomfortable reading this (that's okay; I'm a bit uncomfortable writing it), but if we are to be whole—have integrity and character—we need to understand that the whole includes every aspect of our intellectual, physical, emotional and spiritual well-being. Conducting can take so much out of us that we have little left to give elsewhere. Unfortunately the result can be a very expensive price to pay.

I know of a man who was honored at a retirement party when he left an administrative post in education. After hearing story upon story of this man's kindness, wisdom, humor and caring nature, his grown son addressed the audience. Somewhat stunned and clearly bitter, the son said he did not know the man everyone was talking about; that this wonderful man he had heard about all evening was not the person he knew at home, largely because he had rarely *been* home during all those years.

Imagine being in the room that evening—being this administrator—and realizing how incongruent your life had been: that you had given everything to your job only to leave those closest to you dry.

You have heard it said that no one will ever look back on his life and say "I wish I had spent more time at the office." But I think it is conceivable that a conductor would look back on his life and wish he had conducted that glorious piece or gifted ensemble in that incredible hall or wish he had earned that prestigious honor; or that a music teacher would rationalize almost anything because it had been "for the kids." But when do we cross the line between fulfilling our passion for our art and balancing our lives?

Our choices are not all clear cut. Being a leader takes time and that means time away from the other things in our life, including the important things. We must develop the ability to know when that time is appropriate and when it is not, to know when and how to balance even the most passionate artistry and teaching with the rest of who we are. It is a cliché, I know, this notion of finding a balance—but clichés start as truths that are repeatedly reinforced. The truth of balance is that all life is built on it. You can observe balance as well as imbalance in nature; and when imbalance occurs, problems follow. For us to find balance in our conducting lives means constant re-evaluation, personal discipline and faith that the other elements in our lives are just as important to our effectiveness as conductors as another concert, another class, another score to study or another job. Whole people have a much better chance at doing consistently excellent work with a consistently high level of character. "Leaders who work on achieving career-life balance are not only healthier, but more effective."[104]

Peter Senge said "Personal mastery means approaching one's life

---

104 Cashman, 22.

as a creative work, living life from a creative as opposed to reactive viewpoint."[105] Apply your creativity to the work of art that is your life; your *whole* life.

REMEMBER RULE NUMBER SIX

One of the most interesting books I have read in recent years is *The Art of Possibility* by Rosamund Stone Zander and Boston Philharmonic conductor, Benjamin Zander. One chapter is called Rule Number Six and is about lightening up, not taking yourself so seriously and about the potential for humor to positively impact those we lead.

> Humor and laughter are perhaps the best way we can "get over ourselves." Humor can bring us together around our inescapable foibles, confusions, and miscommunications, and especially over the ways in which we find ourselves acting entitled and demanding, or putting other people down, or flying at each other's throats.[106]

Our character and our ensembles benefit from humor—not the sarcastic, cutting, at-someone-else's-expense kind of commentary but an awareness of the legitimately funny experiences or situations or images that can help us break the hypnosis of seriousness in our daily lives. Humor relaxes the body, connects us to people and recalibrates our perspective toward a more balanced viewpoint. Humor also can reenergize at moments of great tension or effort as described by one of Zander's students in this excerpt from her final white sheet before graduation:

---

105 Peter Senge, quoted in Cashman, 1999, 34.
106 Zander and Zander, 80.

Dear Ben,

You've taught me the different roles humor can play in working with people, relaxing, empowering, freshening. I can remember one rehearsal, close to a December concert, when we were trying to prepare Bartok's Concerto for Orchestra for the performance. It was not going well. I think that many of us, including myself, had taken some standardized test earlier that day, in addition to other rehearsals and coachings in the afternoon. I know that I was mentally exhausted, and we all kept missing notes and entrances. "Take it straight through the second movement," you said to us, "and NO MISTAKES." I don't know about anyone else, but all my muscles tensed, and I wanted nothing more than to run away and crawl into a hole. You must have sensed this, because you thought for a moment and then said, "If you make a mistake ... a five-hundred pound cow will fall on your head." Partly from the image, and partly from the complete surprise of hearing that word out of your mouth, we all began to laugh, and everything was better, including the Bartok. I don't think anything could have relaxed or empowered me more at that moment than the word "cow."[107]

In their research on primal leadership (how leadership works through the emotions), Daniel Goleman, Richard Boyatzis and Annie McKee looked at how emotions and moods impact results.

---

107 Kate Bennett, quoted in Zander and Zander, 2000, 81.

> Although emotions and moods may seem trivial from a business point of view, they have real consequences for getting work done.... While mild anxiety (such as over a looming deadline) can focus attention and energy, prolonged distress can sabotage a leader's relationships and can also hamper work performance by diminishing the brain's ability to process information and respond effectively. A good laugh or an upbeat mood, on the other hand, more often enhances the neural abilities crucial for doing good work.[108]

Humor works like a rubber band, snapping us back to center from a position of rigidity, tension or seriousness. When our lives are out of balance or our rehearsals filled with tension, humor can relax us enough to get the job done and done *better*. "Letting go of our own rigid, external mask brings balance and joy into our life."[109] So, for the sake of your balance and your character and for the sake of your ensemble, remember Rule Number Six.

(By the way, the other rules? There aren't any.)

TAKE TIME TO WITHDRAW

As I write this I am sitting overlooking the waters of Grand Traverse Bay in northern Michigan, a place we vacation each year. It is an easy vacation, centered mostly on beach time and rest as well as reflection—sometimes formal reflection that winds up in written form (like this book) but mostly "think time" reflection, time to get away from people and tasks, responsibilities and details.

---

108 Daniel Goleman, Richard Boyatzis and Annie McKee, "Primal Leadership" in *Business Leadership: A Jossey-Bass Reader* (San Francisco, CA: Jossey-Bass, 2003), 53.

109 Cashman, 165.

Withdrawing from life as we normally live it—the fast paced, scheduled, job-focused life most of us live—is a critical part of developing our character and maintaining our stamina as a leader. Everyone needs time to restock the well, as Julia Cameron[110] phrases it; time to put back *in* some of the energy that gets so quickly and so regularly drained *out* of our bodies, minds and spirits.

When we find ourselves regularly acting defensively, being sarcastic or negative or simply feeling overwhelmed by even the most achievable tasks we are in need of withdrawal time for replenishment. When we are anxious or can no longer see things clearly we have been sucked in too closely to the stuff of life and need to create space in order to regain perspective. When even fun seems like too much to bother about, we need to get away to remember that we really do not carry the entire world on our backs. In short, every leader, to have the energy to lead and the ability to maintain and build our character needs time to withdraw from the people and the tasks in our lives.

This does not mean that you have to wait for summer break to schedule withdrawal time. In fact sometimes there can be so much pressure involved in that one and only vacation with a capital V— all the details of the trip itself, the preparations you need to attend to before you can even leave, the hope that the weather will cooperate—that vacation turns out to be yet another thing to cause you stress.

Withdrawal time needs to happen on a regular basis—every year, to be sure, but in some way withdrawal needs to happen every month, week and day. Withdrawal time is simply time to remove yourself, psychologically and physically (if possible) from your work, mostly, but also even from your family and home responsibilities.

---

110 Julia Cameron has written many wonderful books for artists, all of which I recommend as beneficial for your withdrawal and reflection time.

Leadership in any of its dimensions, from the home to the nation, can be pressure-ridden and very taxing—emotionally and physically. Anyone assuming a leadership obligation needs a strategy in his own defense against this. The best defense is to be able to withdraw, cast off the burden for a while, and relax. This presupposes that one has learned the art of systematic neglect, to sort out the important from the less important and just not to do the less important, even though there may be penalties and censure. It is better to be alive and be censured than to be a dead hero.[111]

No one thinks they have time to get away on a regular basis—certainly not every day. But it is possible if you look for opportunities—even fifteen minutes over a solo cup of coffee before your next appointment or rehearsal. For me, going out to breakfast between the time I get my daughter off to school and have to be in the office is a great time for reflection, recharging and regaining perspective (I also love breakfast). For you it may be closing your office door and giving yourself permission not to answer it when that inevitable knock comes just so you can have some time to yourself. These times of withdrawal are not only times of rest but also times of great inspiration. Many of my insights into musical or leadership problems come to me when I am walking or jogging, sitting on a beach somewhere or just waiting in my van to pick up my daughter from an activity. I often find myself reaching for paper and a pen to write down my thoughts, because that time of withdrawal seems to unlock for me the answers I have been working so hard to find.

---

111 Don M. Frick and Larry C. Spears, ed., *On Becoming a Servant Leader*, San Francisco, Jossey-Bass, 1996, 307.

There's absolutely no way we can get to know ourselves if we don't take some quiet time. How you take time for yourself should fit your lifestyle. For some it may be a 10K run; for others, a quiet walk in the woods. For some it may be watching the sun set; for others, prayer. Whatever you choose to be your form of being alone, find some way of reaching a contemplative state in which you can hear your own voice speaking to you about what truly matters.[112]

Curiously, Greenleaf says burning the candle at both ends is "Okay for a poet or an artist. One's optimum may best be realized that way." It is true that as artists there sometimes comes a flow of creativity that cannot be stopped without forcing an unnatural break in energies and perhaps losing that moment's inspiration and vision for our art. We can get caught up in a cycle of study-rehearsal-performance that seems to pick up creative steam as it goes along, leading to better and better musical results. Work actually *gives* us energy and we happily look for more of it to stoke the creative fires.

"But most who carry responsible roles of leadership should not regulate their lives in that way."[113] The challenge for us as conductors is to remember that we are *both* leaders and artists, making it even more important for us to realize the need to withdraw and balance our artistic drive with our responsibility to see the bigger picture on behalf of the people we lead. We need to become sensitive to the flow of our bodies and our spirits—to go with the energy that art can create in us, but then take the time when we find our well is dry. On the one hand, we must work at knowing when procrastination is keeping us from tapping into the energy our artistic work

---

112 Kouzes and Posner, 66.
113 Greenleaf, in Frick and Spears, 308.

can bring and on the other, become aware of the burnout that can occur when we have gone too many days (or months or years) without time to withdraw and rest.

Leadership is demanding. Leadership demands can only be met if we respect our need to withdraw and learn the art of "systematic neglect." As Mozart wrote: "When I am, as it were, completely myself, entirely alone, and of good cheer—say traveling in a carriage or walking after a good meal... it is on such occasions that ideas flow best and most abundantly."[114] Who are we to argue?

CHARACTER AND THE ARTISTIC PRODUCT

We have explored a lot of ideas in this book, ideas that are aimed at improving who you are as a conductor. But to be this kind of *conductor* means you have to be this kind of *person*. These ideas cannot be put on the same way we put on our concert attire: formally, selectively, to create an appropriate appearance. For us to really be great leaders we have to experience a wholeness, an integrity that means inside and out, on and off the podium, we are the kind of people who carry these principles, attributes and deeply felt beliefs with us always, even if our human nature means we do not always live up to them. Doing follows believing; accomplishing follows desiring. The place to start is to commit ourselves to character evolution and to know the state to which we want to evolve—and let that direct us in our evolution as leading conductors.

When I was younger I worked under a director who did not display many of the character traits we have been talking about in this chapter. He had many holes in his personal and professional life, many ways in which he did not demonstrate ethical behavior or integrity as we have defined them here. Yet his artistic product, our performances, had great integrity. They were authentic, passionate,

---

114 Wolfgang Amadeus Mozart quoted in Cashman, 134.

precise, informed and very musical. For whatever reason there was a kind of purity in this one area of his life that he was able to share with others, though not always in the most humane way. He could be cutting, sarcastic and downright mean precisely as he drilled, instructed and prodded us towards perfection. I put up with this behavior as a young (and intimidated) singer because I wanted to be a part of an excellent ensemble and because there were also good days—days which were actually fun, when I knew I was learning— mixed in with the tyrannical days. Mostly I put up with it because I didn't know any better.

That was many years ago and I have come to think very differently about the entire musical enterprise. I have reflected on how I (mostly unconsciously) adopted some of this conductor's practices in my early career and now regret it, wishing I had understood more about the importance of character, leadership and relationships, and that I had had a role model as a young professional to show me that it was possible to teach for excellence, conduct with passion and achieve a high level of artistry—all with character. I did ultimately work under other conductors who were able to display a balance of character and artistic product and eventually was able to evolve my own style that today I believe displays this balance as well.

But the experience did leave many questions for me: questions about the relationship of *who we are* to *what we do*. Does it really matter?

I believe at a very fundamental level it does. There is a kind of spiritual core that we touch when we conduct, when we are deeply involved with music and with people simultaneously, that reveals ourselves if we are going to be open to the kind of intimacy that music has to offer. That core is our character—our *whole* character, and through it we share who we really are without saying a word or giving a detail. The person who is revealed on the podium is who we really are at a deep level. Even for the best actor, the conductor most adept at keeping on the mask and putting on the appropriate persona, something of the real person comes through when we open ourselves up to the power of music and do this with other people in an equally powerful relationship. And the more powerful the music the more likely the real person will show up on the podium.

I think John Adams had it right when he said "No amount of human having or human doing can make up for a deficit in human being."[115] Character is the greatest talent a conductor can possess, for it is through character that everything else flows. Your strength of character will win over even the most resistant ensembles or aloof audiences and will be the foundation for opening minds to wonderful music. When character is who you are *and* what you do, you have moved to a new level of leadership.

But even the best, most authentic leaders have areas in which they can improve. We might conquer one challenge to our character only to find another appears. We may become consistent in several of our leadership habits but still drag our feet on others. Developing ourselves is a lifelong process, so celebrate the growth along the way and become aware of the incredible ripple effect it has on your life. Then keep going.

---

115 John Adams, quoted in Cashman, 136.

NOT SUPERHEROES,

JUST SUPER WILLING ∽

Reading about character can be incredibly intimidating. After all, who has completely arrived when it comes to developing personal integrity and depth of character? Even the greatest leaders of our lifetime certainly, by virtue of their humanity, struggled with aspects of their character, whether it was apparent or not.

You might think I am painting a picture of a superhero conductor in this book, someone who leaps tall musical obstacles in a single bound, whips out exciting, engaging rehearsal plans from under his cape and comes to the rescue by swooping in to save ensembles and audiences from dangerously boring concerts. (It helps to read that sentence with the Superman theme running in your mind.) While that image is kind of fun to ponder (new reality show, anyone?), it is far from the truth.

We do not have to be superheroes in our quest for character; we just have to be super willing to move further along the continuum of change; being open to new ways of thinking about our approach to working with others; not wearing a persona that puts us artificially above others; taking time to examine our values and how they play out in our everyday behavior, in all spheres of our lives; using humor as a way of connecting to those we touch and as a safeguard against taking ourselves and yes, even our life's work, too seriously. If we are willing to work on character, we can't help but grow in character.

But be warned: as soon as we open ourselves up to growth, there will be challenge. The very nature of growth is adversity, because it is only through adversity that we are forced to change, to think about who we are and what we do. Character is not for cowards but neither is it reserved only for super humans. Somewhere in between are discipline, faith, strength and a willingness to explore what is inside ourselves so we can be of greater service to what is outside ourselves.

Developing character is our greatest challenge, but it is a challenge worth swooping in for. Change into your street clothes and when you come out of that phone booth, go to work. Miracles can happen in the most ordinary of places.

CHAPTER SEVEN

THE JOURNEY CONTINUES:
LEADING FOR THE LONG TERM ~

We started our journey with Maxwell's definition of leadership as influence; we end our journey—at least the journey represented by the pages of this book—with a definition of leadership that expresses what we have explored.

Leadership is authentic self-expression that creates value.[116]

When our profession provides a way for us to express ourselves—and many do not—and when we express ourselves in a way that aligns our goals and skills with our character, we have found an authentic way to "be" in the world. This is rare, I believe, because many people are not fortunate enough to be engaged in an occupation that truly lets them do what they are passionate about, what they are gifted in and what they would spend time doing even if no one paid them (which describes most musicians I have met). The opportunity for authentic self-expression is perhaps nowhere more available than it is in the arts.

Yet we may question the idea of value in this definition of leadership. Sometimes we look around and wonder how much music really matters in the big scheme of things. All this time and effort on something that seems to be an extra, a dispensable, a nice

---

116 Cashman, 20.

occupation but certainly not a noble one. We compare ourselves to doctors—*we don't save lives, do we?*—or to servicemen and women—*we don't protect lives, do we?*—or to cancer researchers—*we don't prolong lives, do we?*

Admittedly what we do as conductors and musicians is a very different sort of mission, but in our own way I do think we save, protect and prolong lives. We save lives from a one-dimensional existence, we protect lives from insensitivity and coldness and we prolong lives by providing a means to know ourselves and others in a deep way and to experience indescribable joy. As conductors we have the opportunity to create rich futures for so many, to teach others so their understanding and artistry grows, to foster relationships that make possible the process of collaborative creating, to inspire others and to become a fully-functioning individual whose character drives all our leadership actions. *Conductors add value to the lives of others*—musicians, students, audiences, congregations, community members and to the culture around us.

Art serves. As conductors we have been given a gift and an opportunity to bring our art to virtually everyone on the planet. Creating, teaching and conducting music are rich gifts that we sometimes forget we have been given: gifts not to keep, but rather to pass on.

We are conductor-*leaders*. As we grow ourselves we grow others, all of us reaching towards something definitely worth pursuing in this lifetime. We strive for greatness, not necessarily defined by accomplishments, notoriety or large audiences but by experiences, relationships and insight. We expend the extra time and energy because we know that our time is precious and if it is going to matter, then striving for greatness is the only option. Sitting on the fence of mediocrity makes no sense, drains our resources and does not represent the music in the way in which it deserves to be represented.

Yes, turning good into great takes energy, but the building of momentum adds more energy back into the pool than it takes out. Conversely, perpetuating mediocrity is an inherently depressing process and drains much more energy out of the pool than it puts back in.[117]

When we get clear about what it means to lead from the podium, we spend time on the things that really matter. We focus our efforts and reap the benefits of that clarity. ME is no longer the end but the catalyst for all the great things that can come to THEM, ultimately to US. We become excited about the opportunity to lead others and do not apologize for striving for excellence because now this quest has been redefined in the direction of those we lead. Our passions are validated, our skills call for ever-increasing sharpening and our dreams begin to be realized.

The journey is never over; it continues as long as we live a life of awareness. But we are encouraged because as we move in the right direction we experience moments of wholeness—glimpses of an integration of self and others, gifts and expression, opportunity and accomplishment. We see what we *can* be—our ensembles, ourselves, our music—and we continue to move toward that goal with our eyes, minds and hearts open to possibility. We keep looking for opportunities to lead from the podium in ways that serve, to be a conductor of character and a teacher with passion. Ultimately what we find is not just meaningful work but a meaningful life.

---

117 Collins, 208.

THE GREATEST LEADER ～つ

You may have wondered why, after all these pages about leadership, I have not even mentioned the man who many consider to be the greatest leader of all time: Jesus of Nazareth.

I suppose I have been cautious, not wanting to alienate those of you who would resist spirituality of any kind from creeping into a book that was supposed to be about your professional life— well, mostly. But just as many others writing about leadership these days, I have found it is impossible to separate ourselves into parts, some reserved for work and others of a more personal nature. When it comes to developing ourselves as leaders we need to think about the whole person we are and how that person interacts with the rest of the world. More and more, the notion of spirituality in the workplace is showing up in books, seminars and courses on leadership even in the most secular of places. So it is only appropriate for our purposes to consider the life and work of Jesus as we develop our own understanding of what it means to be a leader.

Jesus was many things and did many things on this earth. Whatever religious beliefs you may hold, history tells us Jesus was a great *teacher*, helping people grow as he masterfully shared ideas with people of all backgrounds and abilities. He was a powerful *leader*, founding the most significant belief system in the history of humanity. He *worked miracles*, large and small, and he *served others*, even when his fame and admiration made it awkward if not shockingly countercultural to perform many of the acts of service attributed to him such as washing the feet of his followers. Eventually he sacrificed everything in the ultimate act of service to those he led.

Jesus was a *catalyst for change*. He fully used his skills, opportunities, passion and brief moment in time to make what many believe to be an unparalleled difference in the world. As an example of leadership, what can we learn from this?

We exist in a *place* in *time*, among *people* and with a *skill set* and *personality characteristics* that we can use to change the lives of those around us. We are charged with a job and we have opportunities and often, the position, title or authority to make a difference. I have become more and more aware of my ability to enact change and have begun to enthusiastically look for opportunities to extend myself on behalf of others which, I must admit, is a very different way of looking at life than I had in my younger days as a conductor, teacher, administrator, leader and yes, person. Whereas I used to enjoy my own accomplishments I now find more satisfaction in seeing others grow in some way, knowing I had a role in making that happen—that by using my influence I was able to serve someone else and in the end, take part in experiencing a bounty of benefits that even I could not envision. It is weird and wonderful, really—a kind of out-of-body experience that makes life so much richer than just trying to be a well-respected musician.

Whatever your religious beliefs, studying Jesus' life and impact as a leader is worth your time. His life can be an encouragement for your own and can provide direction as you begin to unveil the possibility that exists in your own time on this planet.

A CLEARER VISION FOR INFLUENCE ∼

Every summer during our vacation in northern Michigan I re-read Anne Morrow Lindbergh's *A Gift from the Sea*, a classic book still relevant some fifty years after it was first written. One of the things that always amazes me when I read the opening pages is realizing that the author did not start out to write a book for others to learn from; she just used her writing to work out her own thoughts—to journal, reflect on her life and chart a course for its next stage. When she shared these ideas with others she was surprised to find out that her struggles, her curiosities, her musings—so individual and personal, it seemed—were really the struggles, curiosities and musings of so many others.

> I found that my point of view was not unique. In varying settings and under different forms, I discovered that many women, and men, too, were grappling with essentially the same questions as I, and were hungry to discuss and argue and hammer out possible answers. Even those whose lives had appeared to be ticking imperturbably under their smiling clock-faces were often trying, like me, to evolve another rhythm with more creative pauses in it, more adjustment to their individual needs, and new and more alive relationships to themselves as well as others.[118]

---

118   Anne Morrow Lindbergh, *Gift From the Sea*, New York: Pantheon Books, 1955, 10–11.

My exploration into leadership started out in a similar way. My classes, rehearsals, articles, workshops and now, this book began as explorations of ideas and experiments in applying those ideas to my own life. But I, too, have found as Anne Morrow Lindbergh did that I am not alone in my thinking or my challenges or my desires; that many people who have claimed conducting as their chosen profession also struggle and wonder and reflect and experiment as they move forward on a path to becoming a better leader.

I have explored a lot of ideas in this book; ideas that may have been new to you or that may have been reminders of values and beliefs buried by years of work and busyness. Hopefully you have found some encouragement and inspiration in these pages, but even more I hope you will ask yourself the question "What can I *do* with these ideas? How can I embrace them so they make a difference in my life and the lives of those I lead?"

The clue is in the word "do." *Do* something that reflects your clearer understanding of the kind of vision needed for your organization to thrive. Do something that will build a better trust relationship between you and the musicians in your ensemble. Do something to become a better teacher, one who recognizes the importance of invested, engaged, empowered musicians. Do something that moves you from coercion to persuasion and that grows your character in significant ways. Whatever you do that takes these ideas and puts them into action will take you one step closer to making a difference.

"To make a difference" has always been my final course goal on every syllabus, whether written for an ensemble, a methods class or a conducting class. Even years before I began studying leadership formally I sensed that *what life comes down to is using our influence in a positive way, making a change that will document that we have been here.* It is all about realizing our place in this world—not just geographically but professionally—about serving and taking seriously the charge to bloom where you are planted. You may be a part-time conductor in a small school or a full-time conductor in a very visible professional organization. In a real sense it doesn't matter what your position is; there are audiences to perform for and music to be shared; there are personalities to win over and hearts to touch. Whether you stay in a position for a year or your entire career, making a difference means using that time to influence people in the best way possible. Lead them by teaching them well; create a vision for the organization that can inspire them to excellence; work to develop relationships built on trust; use your passion to persuade them to move to the next level; and be by example the kind of person that displays these abilities as integral parts of your character.

This is our charge, our privilege and our responsibility as leaders from the podium. All eyes are on us. Let us use our time well.

"For, in the end, it is impossible to have a great life unless it is a meaningful life. And it is very difficult to have a meaningful life without meaningful work. Perhaps, then, you might gain that rare tranquility that comes from knowing that you've had a hand in creating something of intrinsic excellence that makes a contribution. Indeed, you might even gain that deepest of all satisfactions: knowing that your short time here on this earth has been well spent, and that it mattered."[119]

---

119 Collins, 210.

ABOUT THE AUTHOR ~

Dr. Ramona M. Wis has been a conductor, teacher, and performer for thirty years, leading musicians of all ages in educational, professional and volunteer organizations. Currently, she is the Mimi Rolland Professor in the Fine Arts and Chair of the Department of Music at North Central College in Naperville, Illinois, where she conducts the North Central College Women's Chorale and teaches courses in conducting, methods, and servant leadership. Dr. Wis has also served on the faculties of Northwestern University, Northern Illinois University and various public schools and holds several degrees, including a Ph.D. from Northwestern University. She has held leadership positions in several professional organizations, including that of President of the American Choral Directors Association in Illinois, and has sung under Robert Shaw, Margaret Hillis and James Levine. Dr. Wis presents workshops and lectures on leadership and is active as a clinician, guest conductor, public speaker, and author. She lives in suburban Chicago with her husband and daughter, and their dogs Maggie and Fred.